Anti-social behaviour strategies

This publication can be provided in alternative formats, such as large print, Braille, audiotape and on disk. Please contact: Communications Department, Joseph Rowntree Foundation, The Homestead, 40 Water End, York YO30 6WP. Tel: 01904 615905. Email: info@jrf.org.uk

Anti-social behaviour strategies

Finding a balance

Andrew Millie, Jessica Jacobson, Eraina McDonald and Mike Hough

First published in Great Britain in June 2005 by

The Policy Press
Fourth Floor, Beacon House
Queen's Road
Bristol BS8 1QU
UK

Tel no +44 (0)117 331 4054
Fax no +44 (0)117 331 4093
E-mail tpp-info@bristol.ac.uk
www.policypress.org.uk

Published for the Joseph Rowntree Foundation by The Policy Press

ISBN 1 86134 763 4

British Library Cataloguing in Publication Data
A catalogue record for this book is available from the British Library.

Library of Congress Cataloging-in-Publication Data
A catalog record for this book has been requested.

This project was undertaken by the Institute for Criminal Policy Research (ICPR) at the School of Law, King's College London. **Dr Andrew Millie** was at the ICPR but is now Senior Researcher at the Policy Research Institute and Senior Lecturer in the School of Legal Studies, University of Wolverhampton. **Dr Jessica Jacobson** is an independent consultant. **Eraina McDonald** was a Research Assistant at the ICPR and **Mike Hough** is Professor of Criminal Policy and Director of the ICPR.

The **Joseph Rowntree Foundation** has supported this project as part of its programme of research and innovative development projects, which it hopes will be of value to policy makers, practitioners and service users. The facts presented and views expressed in this report are, however, those of the authors and not necessarily those of the Foundation.

Cover design by Qube Design Associates, Bristol
Printed in Great Britain by Hobbs the Printers Ltd, Southampton

Contents

Acknowledgements

We are very grateful to the Joseph Rowntree Foundation for supporting this project as part of its Housing and Neighbourhoods programme of research. The facts presented and views expressed in this report are, however, those of the authors and not necessarily those of the Foundation.

We would like to thank the various police, local authority and other statutory and voluntary workers from the three case-study areas who were enormously helpful and gave their time freely. Thanks are also due to the residents of the case-study areas who were interviewed or were involved in focus group discussions. We are also grateful for the advice and support provided by our advisory group: Nicola Bacon, Professor Adam Crawford, John Graham, Simon Harding, Dr Barrie Irving, Andy Mills, Bill Pitt, Gill Strachan and Mike Thomas. Thanks are also due to Katharine Knox and other staff at the Joseph Rowntree Foundation for their help and support throughout the project's lifetime.

Summary

- Anti-social behaviour (ASB) has a significant impact on the lives of a minority of people in Britain, particularly in areas of social deprivation and inner cities. But it has little or no effect on the quality of life of the majority of the population.
- The general population tends to equate ASB with problems they associate with young people, including graffiti, drug use or simple rowdiness. Two-thirds favour preventive action over tough action against ASB perpetrators.
- In the local neighbourhoods, people were mainly concerned with three issues: general misbehaviour by children and young people; visible drug and alcohol misuse; and neighbour disputes and 'problem families'.
- Residents often regarded ASB as a symptom of social and moral decline. Local agencies tended to explain it in terms of social exclusion – especially of young people from deprived backgrounds. Some people, however, thought that much of the behaviour now labelled as ASB simply showed that 'kids will be kids'.
- These different perspectives on ASB implied different solutions. Those who saw it as a consequence of declining moral standards tended to favour tougher discipline. Those who saw it as a result of deprivation preferred prevention and inclusion.
- In all three case-study sites, local ASB strategies have been adopted that balance enforcement with preventive work, and emphasise the need for a graduated and proportionate approach to enforcement. This contrasts with the stronger national emphasis on enforcement.

We conclude that both national and local ASB strategies should aim for a balance between enforcement and prevention and that more care is needed in defining ASB and in deciding the limits on the use of civil remedies.

Views on ASB: the national picture

For most people in Britain, ASB is not a big problem: 61% of respondents to the 2003/04 British Crime Survey (BCS), for example, reported no bad effects from any of 16 types of ASB. On the other hand, ASB is an acute concern for a significant *minority* of people. Rowdy teenagers in the street had a fairly or very big effect on the lives of one in five respondents to an Office for National Statistics (ONS) survey commissioned for this study. Anti-social behaviour tends to be concentrated in deprived urban areas: a third (34%) of BCS respondents in inner-city areas thought levels of ASB were high in their area.

ASB can take many forms. Youth ASB appears to be the most visible and worrisome. For example, 27% of ONS respondents said that rowdy teenagers on the street or youths hanging around were the worst forms of ASB where they lived. Interestingly, adults under the age of 45 were more concerned about youth ASB than their elders – perhaps because they were more likely to experience this kind of ASB. The ONS survey showed that other forms of ASB, such as vandalism or litter/rubbish, had a smaller impact on people's lives – although a larger proportion of the population were exposed to these less serious problems.

Asked about methods of tackling ASB, people were more likely to opt for 'preventive action to deal with the causes' than 'tough action against perpetrators'. Only 20% chose the latter, compared with 66% who opted for preventive action and 11% who favoured both.

ASB in three case-study neighbourhoods

Three case-study sites were chosen for further study in order to learn more about local views on the experience of ASB, possible causes of the problems and potential solutions. The neighbourhoods were selected on the basis of their high levels of ASB and apparently contrasting local strategies for tackling it. It turned out that the similarities in the local ASB strategies were greater than the differences between them. In all three areas, graduated enforcement strategies culminating in the deployment of Anti-Social Behaviour Orders (ASBOs) were combined with a range of preventive measures undertaken by different agencies, some funded through mainstream services and others through special initiatives.

Interviews and focus groups were organised with residents and ASB practitioners in each site. In all three neighbourhoods, issues relating to children and young people caused particular concern. Residents and practitioners spoke about boisterous and rowdy behaviour by children; young people congregating; young people causing damage to property and the environment; and the anti-social use of cars and motorbikes by children and young people. People were also concerned about drug and alcohol misuse, and the impact of neighbour disputes and 'problem families'.

Focus groups with residents showed how exposure to ASB can provoke a profound sense of powerlessness and lack of control over the social environment. People had real concerns about retaliation if they intervened, and felt that the statutory agencies were largely impotent in the face of serious misbehaviour by young people. This sense of powerlessness appeared to be both a consequence of ASB and a cause, as it increased the chances that worsening ASB would go unchecked.

Explaining and responding to ASB: three narratives

When talking about the *causes* of local ASB problems, respondents largely focused on issues relating to young people. They tended to provide explanations that were rooted in broader conceptions of social and cultural change. Three main strands of thought, or 'narratives of ASB', emerged in what was said – although these are by no means mutually exclusive or discrete:

1) **Social and moral decline:** problems of ASB were seen as symptoms of wider social and cultural change – more specifically, a decline in moral standards and family values.
2) **Disengaged youth and families:** ASB was thought to be rooted in the increasing disengagement from wider society of a significant minority of children and young people and (in many cases) their families.
3) **'Kids will be kids':** ASB was seen as a reflection of the age-old tendency for young people to get into trouble, challenge boundaries and antagonise their elders.

The first two narratives assume that problems of ASB are getting worse, because of a generalised process of decline or because of the increasing disengagement of a minority of British youth and/or their families. The third narrative does not assume that problems of ASB are necessarily getting worse in themselves, but suggests that the *context* of youthful misbehaviour is changing, and as a result people are more likely to perceive young people's behaviour as anti-social and to worry about it. To some extent, the narratives play out tensions between younger and older generations – with the older generation more likely to articulate the first (and possibly the second) narrative, and the younger generation to suggest the third. In contrast, ASB practitioners with social welfare and support roles tended to favour the second narrative and, to a lesser extent, the third.

Those who viewed ASB as an issue of social and moral decline were often highly cynical about the effectiveness of the new range of provisions for tackling it, such as ASBOs and dispersal orders. However, they also saw little hope in alternative approaches other than, possibly, community mobilisation against ASB perpetrators. For those who largely viewed ASB in terms of the 'disengagement' of certain young people and their families, early intervention of a preventive nature, intensive youth work and community partnership were thought to offer the most promise. From this perspective, enforcement was necessary but had to be used selectively and with great care. The 'kids will be kids' narrative implied that diversionary activities for young people should be the cornerstone of local ASB strategies.

Implications for ASB policy and practice

The study points to various lessons for policy and practice:

- the search for solutions to ASB;
- the management of local action on ASB; and
- the handling of public opinion.

The search for solutions

The Home Office TOGETHER campaign – with its implicit call for higher standards and tougher discipline to address ASB – points clearly towards a causal narrative of social and moral decline. On the other hand, the fact that problems of ASB are concentrated most heavily in areas facing [illegible] to prioritise enforcement at a national level, and concerns about the risks of enforcement, and commitment to preventive options, at local levels. Local practitioners who participated in this study stressed the intractability of problems of disorder in deprived areas. They did not talk about ASB simply as a problem of perpetrators preying on the 'law-abiding majority' – but as forms of conflict within communities with limited capacity for self-regulation. They regarded the perpetrators as young people with limited personal resources, living in areas offering limited opportunities. Not surprisingly, they tended to see enforcement as only one element within the set of remedies needed to rebuild these communities. They thought that enforcement tactics could provide a short-term solution to ASB, but that, for the longer term, enforcement clearly needed to be balanced with inclusionary measures in order to encourage a disenfranchised section of society to feel that they had a stake in it again.

In areas most beset by ASB, ways have to be found of countering the sense of powerlessness and accompanying entrenched pessimism among residents. There is a need to break the vicious circle whereby fears and expectations of ASB, fear of retaliation, lack of faith in the authorities' capacity to do anything and incidents of ASB all reinforce each other. Visible enforcement action may provide the leverage to do so, although it seems likely that measures for building community capacity are also needed.

The national TOGETHER initiative is a time-limited campaign, intended to respond to public concerns, to reduce public preparedness to tolerate ASB, to increase public expectations about the level of response from local authorities and police, and to spur these agencies into action. To communicate these messages clearly, TOGETHER has used simple, populist language, justifying tough enforcement. As localities respond and adapt to evolving circumstances, it may be that the national approach will also need to shift further in acknowledgement of the potential benefits of a more balanced response to the issue that considers both victims and perpetrators.

The management of local action on ASB

It is important to develop shared definitions of ASB. The TOGETHER campaign tended to avoid doing so, not wishing to curb artificially the range of uses to which the new measures for tackling ASB could be put. Now that the need for action against ASB is more widely accepted, it is time for agencies to be clearer about the ambit of the term ASB. The main reason for this is simple: if local authorities and police put in place strategies for dealing with ASB, they need to commit resources to these strategies, clarify responsibilities across agencies and manage the performance of those delivering the strategies. This cannot be done unless there is clarity about where ASB begins and ends.

There are other reasons for taking care with definitions. The new ASB remedies include some sweeping powers. Civil law measures such as ASBOs supplement the criminal law system of deterrent threat with personalised deterrent threats tailor-made to specific perpetrators. If the threats are ignored, the penalty can be heavy. It is important to develop much more explicit rationales for justifying the deployment of such powerful civil law remedies – in order to set agreed limits to their use.

The handling of public opinion on ASB

The government's TOGETHER campaign appeals to the narrative of declining standards, and encourages the 'law-abiding majority' to take a stand against ASB. It offers images of the struggle between ordinary decent folk and a tide of loutishness. In reality, the factors that underlie ASB are likely to involve a complex interaction of social and economic policies that have borne down hard on Britain's most disadvantaged communities. It is important to avoid an oversimplified political and media debate about ASB.

As a means of mobilising agencies to action, the TOGETHER campaign has much to recommend itself. The public presentation of the campaign:

- resonates with real public anxieties about declining standards;
- cogently reshapes these worries into a sense of vulnerability in the face of pressing threats to social order; and
- presents the image of tough, resolute government action responding to these threats.

On the other hand, there are minuses. Fuelling public concerns about social order in this way pays off only if the tough, resolute response is fully persuasive. However, the 'declining standards' narrative is infused with a deep sense of pessimism about the scope for solutions of any sort, and in particular a well-entrenched cynicism about the likelihood of an effective response from local agencies. The media and presentational elements of the TOGETHER campaign could succeed in fuelling public anxieties and playing on existing fears, but fail to present a persuasive government response. The government might do better to present its ASB strategies in ways that recognise the need to be not only tough on ASB but tough on the causes of ASB.

1

Introduction

In England and Wales, politicians and practitioners have since 1997 paid increasing attention to what has become known as 'anti-social behaviour' (henceforth ASB). The term is usually used to cover minor crimes and near-criminal behaviour that cause public annoyance, anxiety and disruption to daily life. The government has introduced a range of new powers for tackling those problems of ASB that cause greatest concern to the general public. At local levels, key agencies are making ever-greater use of these powers, and are placing a heavy emphasis on ASB within the wider community safety agenda.

This study was set up to advance strategic thinking on ASB. Through empirical research – combining a national survey with in-depth fieldwork in three neighbourhoods experiencing high levels of ASB – we have aimed to develop principles for effective ASB responses. This introductory chapter sets out the context of the research. We address the problem of defining ASB and consider why and how ASB has emerged as a policy issue in Britain. The chapter ends with a discussion of our research methods.

Defining ASB

ASB is a difficult concept to define. Definitions in statute are very broad: the 1998 Crime and Disorder Act, which introduced Anti-Social Behaviour Orders (ASBOs), defines ASB as behaviour that 'caused or was likely to cause harassment, alarm or distress to one or more persons not of the same household as [the perpetrator]'. Legislation obviously favours inclusiveness, but as an analytic definition this is unhelpfully vague (see Jacobson et al, forthcoming). While it excludes domestic incidents, it potentially encompasses all other forms of behaviour that cause offence.

Behaviour usually viewed as ASB lies on a spectrum of misbehaviours from those that are too minor to merit intervention by the authorities to those that are so serious as to demand criminal prosecution. The difficulty, in conceptual terms, is in defining how and where to draw the boundaries between ASB and minor incivilities at one end of the spectrum, and ASB and serious crime at the other end of the spectrum. In practice, subjective factors necessarily play a large part in determining where the boundaries lie: in other words, the treatment of certain incidents as ASB depends on their perceived impact on the victim. Decisions made on the ground about what is and is not ASB are also partly shaped by pragmatic factors – that is, by the usefulness and applicability of ASB remedies (or, alternatively, criminal prosecution) in the circumstances of a given case.

The Home Office, in developing its TOGETHER campaign against ASB, has tended to avoid grappling with conceptual definitions of ASB. The tone of official statements often implies that anyone of good sense can recognise ASB – or 'yob behaviour' as it is typically described.[1] A recent Home Office document has offered a 'typology of anti-social behaviour', which is intended to 'provide a practical framework and guide to the main categories of behaviour that are widely accepted to be anti-social by both practitioners and the public' (Harradine et al, 2004, p 4). The typology, which was used to structure the Home Office 'one-day count' of ASB

[1] For example, as by Home Office Minister Hazel Blears, quoted in Home Office press notice 096/2004, concerning the launch of the TOGETHER Actionline and Academy.

in September 2003, lists specific types of ASB under four main headings:

- misuse of public space;
- disregard for community/personal well-being;
- acts directed at people;
- environmental damage.

In our own previous work on ASB, we have concluded that conceptual clarity in the definition of ASB is important, and not just an academic indulgence. One reason for taking definitional care is that some ASB remedies such as ASBOs can powerfully curb the freedoms of those on whom they are imposed, and it is important to be clear about the limits to the use of such powers. A second reason is that tackling ASB effectively requires strategic thinking and partnership work – which in turn demand that the agencies involved are clear about the problems they are addressing and the aims they are seeking to achieve. We therefore developed a working definition that makes explicit the rationale for responding to certain kinds of incidents as ASB.[2] This defined ASB as behaviour that:

- causes harassment, alarm or distress
- to individuals not of the same household as the perpetrator, such that
- it requires interventions from the relevant authorities; **but**
- criminal prosecution and punishment may be inappropriate
- because the individual components of the behaviour:
  - are not prohibited by the criminal law **or**
  - in isolation, constitute relatively minor offences.

This definition recognises that ASB often, but not always, constitutes harassment, alarm or distress by virtue of the *cumulative* impact of repeated incidents that in isolation may not be a serious concern. We readily admit that this definition is still open to interpretation; however, it usefully narrows the focus to that family of behaviours that can in aggregate be appallingly intrusive into people's lives, without being particularly serious breaches of standards when considered on a case-by-case basis. Within our proposed definition of ASB, we feel it is useful to distinguish between three main forms of ASB, as set out in Box 1, below.

The emergence of ASB as a policy issue

ASB has emerged as a policy priority in Britain against a background of long-standing academic interest in the subject. In the US in particular, researchers have since the 1960s been exploring the links between physical and social

Box 1: The main forms of ASB

Interpersonal/malicious ASB is behaviour directed against specific individuals or groups, eg:

- intimidation/threats by neighbours
- minor violence
- hoax calls
- vandalism directed at individuals or groups
- serious verbal abuse (eg, directed at public sector workers)

Environmental ASB is behaviour that – deliberately or through carelessness – degrades the local environment, such as:

- dog-fouling
- setting fire to rubbish
- noise nuisance
- graffiti (eg, on the transport network)
- abandoned vehicles
- littering/fly-tipping

ASB restricting use of shared space refers to threatening or physically obstructive behaviours that stop people using shared spaces, such as:

- intimidating behaviour by groups of youths
- drug abuse in public places
- street drinking/drunkenness
- soliciting and kerb-crawling
- obstructive/inconsiderate use of vehicles

[2] This definition was developed through collaborative work with the strategic agencies responsible for tackling ASB in London (see GLA, 2004; see also Millie et al, forthcoming).

environments and perceived levels of crime and disorder (for example, Jacobs, 1961; Newman, 1972). The 'broken windows' thesis, developed by Wilson and Kelling (1982; see also Kelling and Coles, 1996), has been especially influential. Wilson and Kelling argued that low-level incidents of disorder or minor signs of neighbourhood decline (such as broken windows) can damage public confidence and exacerbate fear of crime; over the longer term they can disempower local communities and contribute to rising crime.

Other researchers have further developed the 'broken windows' thesis. Skogan (1986, 1990), for example, has analysed the part that social and physical disorder can play in generating neighbourhood decline. Many of the ideas about the links between disorder, crime and neighbourhood decline have been put into practice in the Chicago Alternative Policing Strategy (CAPS) – a large-scale community policing programme introduced in 1993 and extensively evaluated (see, for example, Skogan and Hartnett, 1997; Skogan et al, 2002, 2004). This has shown that the police can achieve close engagement with at least some communities, and that responsive policing can result in both increased confidence in the police and reduced concern about neighbourhood problems.

Sampson and colleagues (Sampson et al, 1997; Sampson and Raudenbush, 1999) have explored similar themes, but reached somewhat different conclusions. On the basis of research also conducted in Chicago, they have argued that public disorder is not causally linked to crime, but that disorder and most crimes are "explained by the same constructs at the neighborhood level" (Sampson and Raudenbush, 1999, p 637). They cite structural disadvantage (particularly poverty) and a lack of 'collective efficacy' as causes of both crime and disorder.

For Sampson and Raudenbush, collective efficacy is about the existence of mutual trust and solidarity among residents of a local area, and the consequent capacity of residents to intervene in social situations for the common good. The issue of collective efficacy is of particular interest also to other researchers who have explored disorder and ASB. Skogan (1990), for example, argues that social disorganisation and the associated lack of informal control, along with structural problems such as inequality, are root causes of problems of disorder. Phillips and Smith (2003) have looked at how normal or positive interpersonal contact contributes to the building or maintenance of a civil society. They cite the work of Putnam (1994) who suggests that improvements in 'the nature and quantity of face-to-face interactions' can help rebuild the apparent decline in civic and community activity and make crime prevention strategies more workable (Phillips and Smith, 2003, p 87). From this perspective, ASB is likely to be reduced in areas where residents have the capacity to act as 'capable guardians' of their neighbourhoods.[3]

Why is ASB a priority today?

The priority accorded to ASB in Britain today can be explained in a variety of ways. One view is that current problems of ASB reflect the broad cultural shifts that Britain has undergone over the past 50 years. For example, the loss of a sense of community in many areas, a decline in deference and the greater emphasis on individualism and consumerist values have all had repercussions on standards of civil behaviour. More specific social developments are also relevant here, such as increasing levels of binge drinking and use of illicit drugs. From this perspective, it is easy to see why New Labour has been attracted to a civil renewal agenda (see Blunkett, 2003).

But it is equally important to bear in mind the contribution to problems of ASB made by five decades of social and economic policy. Levels of ASB tend to be highest in inner cities, poor council estates and other low-income areas (Thorpe and Wood, 2004) – the kinds of neighbourhoods worst affected by the decline in the industrial and manufacturing base over the 1970s and 1980s. Housing policies that have allowed large concentrations of poor, socially excluded families have often also exacerbated problems in these areas. It can be argued that many social and economic developments over the past half-century have had the effect of stripping these areas of their social capital.

[3] Routine activity theory dictates that crimes occur when there is an interaction between a motivated offender, an attractive target and a lack of capable guardianship (Cohen and Felson, 1979; Felson, 1998). While it is conceivable that the same would apply to some ASB, it is often the perpetrator's *lack* of motivation to do anything better that can lead to ASB.

If such developments have created the preconditions for the emergence of ASB problems, local and central government criminal justice policies are also implicated. In the 1980s in particular, many local authorities and the police regarded each other with grave suspicion. Many councils established 'police monitoring groups', whose aim was more to contain or even subvert police activity than to support it. While ASB was an issue at that time, relations between the police and city councils were often so fractured that it was impossible to mount any effective action to counter it.

The 1990s saw a welcome bringing together of the police and local government – as exemplified in the development of crime and disorder reduction partnerships (CDRPs). However, central government initiatives to tackle crime have been at the expense of action against ASB. Policing has always involved a balance between crime fighting and order maintenance. Since the mid-1990s, successive governments have followed a modernisation agenda that has imposed performance management targets on the police that have skewed their function towards crime control (Hough, 2003, 2004). Performance management regimes in the mid- and late-1990s prioritised 'volume crime' (such as burglary and car crime) and implicitly removed priority from individually less serious incidents of ASB (see FitzGerald et al, 2002).

The hole in provision was initially filled by local authority housing officers or registered social landlords whose agenda, understandably, was predominantly to remove perpetrators of serious ASB from their properties. From 2000, neighbourhood warden schemes run by local authorities, or under the umbrella of CDRPs, were also introduced and funded directly from central government through the Department of the Environment, Transport and the Regions (now the Office of the Deputy Prime Minister). Their remit was to focus on minor environmental crime and public reassurance.

In 2001 the police reform White Paper highlighted high levels of public concern about disorder, and the critical importance of the police's role in helping to 'support decent civil communities' and addressing 'more minor social issues' (Home Office, 2001, p 84). The first National Policing Plan (Home Office, 2002) likewise emphasised the need for effective action against ASB. Consequently, current policing policy now also covers the policing of disorder – as exemplified in the National Reassurance Policing Programme[4] and the introduction of Police Community Support Officers (PCSOs). The latest policing White Paper (Home Office 2004a, p 7) emphasises the importance of neighbourhood policing, which involves:

> ... dedicated teams of police officers, community support officers and wardens providing a visible, reassuring presence, preventing and detecting crime and developing a constructive and lasting engagement with members of their community.

The TOGETHER campaign

Today, tackling ASB is high on the government's agenda. The Home Office TOGETHER campaign, along with the introduction of a wide range of new powers for responding to ASB through a series of Acts of Parliament,[5] can be seen as part of an exercise in *rebalancing* systems of social control. The TOGETHER campaign was launched in autumn 2003, followed in early 2004 with a series of roadshows, the establishment of an ASB 'Action Line' and an ASB 'Academy' of practitioners. In the words of the TOGETHER website (www.together.gov.uk), it is 'a campaign across England and Wales that takes a stand against anti-social behaviour and puts the needs of the local community first'. This 'no nonsense' rhetoric has continued with the publication of the Home Office's five-year strategic plan in July 2004. As part of an agenda to 'put the interests of the law-abiding citizen first', the plan is that, by 2008, the Home Office will have in place:

---

[4] The development of the reassurance programme has been partly informed by the 'signal crimes perspective' of researchers Innes and Fielding (eg, Innes, 2004; Innes and Fielding, 2002). Their contention is that residents' reactions to local 'signal' incidents determine whether they fear crime. Signal incidents may range from serious crimes to ASB incidents. Once identified, signal incidents can be countered by 'control signals' that reassure the public. (See also Millie and Herrington, 2005; and www.reassurancepolicing.co.uk.)

[5] The most significant of which, in terms of ASB, is the 2003 Anti-Social Behaviour Act.

> [a] no-tolerance approach to anti-social behaviour, with new powers for the police, such as curfews, specialist prosecutors and anti-social behaviour response courts, and support for communities. (Home Office, 2004b, p 10)

This is a two-pronged approach based on enforcement and support for communities, although in the first year of the TOGETHER campaign, enforcement appears to be in the driving seat. In the words of the Prime Minister, 'We've given you the powers, and it's time to use them' (Blair, 2003). The language is all about action: ASB is seen as something that is always unacceptable and demands tough and immediate responses (see also Hough and Jacobson, 2004). If the criminal justice system is too slow – or too lenient – then the new civil powers are there to step in, as Tony Blair noted in the same speech at the launch of the TOGETHER campaign:

> First, ASB is for many [on estates] the number one item of concern right on their doorstep – the graffiti, vandalism, dumped cars, drug dealers in the street, abuse from truanting school-age children. Secondly, though many of these things are in law a criminal offence, it is next to impossible for the police to prosecute without protracted court process, bureaucracy and hassle, when conviction will only result in a minor sentence. Hence these new powers to take swift, summary action. (Blair, 2003)

Many of the issues being addressed through government policy on ASB are also at the heart of other wide-ranging and ambitious government programmes. Most obviously, perhaps, ASB issues have direct relevance to the Home Office programmes on civil renewal and community cohesion (which are promoting a greater sense of citizenship and stronger communities) and the neighbourhood renewal strategy (which is seeking to narrow the gap between deprived neighbourhoods and the rest of the country). In particular, the theme of community engagement is common to these different strands of government policy. However, the focus on enforcement and short-term action within policy on ASB sometimes appears at odds with the emphases on community cohesion and long-term planning within the neighbourhood renewal and civil renewal agendas.

Aims and methods of the study

Despite the resources that have been dedicated – at national and local levels – to designing and implementing new measures for tackling ASB, strategists and policy makers have tended not to spell out precisely why it is that ASB needs to be addressed more vigorously today than in the past. It is taken for granted that ASB can cause enormous problems for individuals and for neighbourhoods, but the nature and impact of these problems have not been examined systematically or in detail. Similarly, while responses to ASB have been developed with great urgency, this very urgency sometimes means that not much thought has been put into determining what *kinds* of responses are needed in different contexts, and why.

This study set out to fill some of these gaps in understanding. More precisely, our main aim was to **develop general principles for effective local and national responses to ASB**. We sought to develop these principles through an analysis of:

- views of ASB among the general public and those living in areas of high ASB; and
- experiences and perceptions of ASB among practitioners and local service managers engaged in community safety and related work.

In order to investigate views among the general public, we undertook a national survey of attitudes to ASB, and carried out focus groups and interviews with residents in three neighbourhoods selected as case-study sites. In the same neighbourhoods, we conducted interviews with practitioners and local managers, and set these in context by looking at the range of ASB-related initiatives being undertaken in these areas.

The survey

We commissioned a suite of questions in the monthly Office for National Statistics (ONS) omnibus national survey. This is the only omnibus survey in the UK that offers a true probability sample of the population aged 16 or over, and it typically achieves a response rate of around 65%. Seventeen questions on ASB were included in the April 2004 ONS survey, which had a sample size of 1,678. These questions (listed in Appendix A) explored respondents' views on the nature of ASB and the problems it causes, and methods of tackling ASB. In analysing the ONS findings, we have looked also at findings of other relevant attitudinal research.

Research in three neighbourhoods

In the three case-study neighbourhoods, we carried out qualitative, micro-level research. In each site, we undertook the following:

a) Three or four focus groups with residents, exploring experiences of ASB and views on local initiatives. These groups, which were organised by a recruitment consultancy, comprised young men and women aged 16 to 18; parents of young children and teenagers; and men and women over the age of retirement.
b) Semi-structured interviews with representatives of local community associations, who were also local residents. These interviews again focused on the respondents' experiences of ASB, and also explored the ways in which residents can be active partners in local initiatives on ASB.
c) Semi-structured interviews with officers from key agencies, including ASB coordinators, police officers, wardens, housing officers, Youth Offending Team (YOT) representatives, community safety officers and Sure Start workers. Around 20-25 such interviews were conducted in each site, exploring perceptions of local ASB problems and the scope and impact of local initiatives.
d) Reviews of relevant policy and strategy documents.

In total, we interviewed 73 respondents on a one-to-one basis, and conducted 10 focus groups involving a total of 85 individuals. All interviews and focus groups were taped and transcribed. The transcripts were then subjected to thematic analysis.

The case-study sites

Each of the three neighbourhoods in which we conducted our fieldwork covered one to two local authority wards. Our original criteria for selection of these neighbourhoods as case-study sites were that:

a) they should be located in different regions;
b) each should have features – such as relatively high crime levels and levels of deprivation – commonly associated with ASB problems;
c) each should have distinctive and contrasting ASB strategies.

The three neighbourhoods we selected met the first two criteria. Our initial view was that the areas also represented contrasting approaches to ASB, ranging from enforcement-focused to prevention-oriented. Over the course of the fieldwork, however, it emerged that the three neighbourhoods' ASB strategies were more similar than we had originally judged. In all three areas, agencies were undertaking a variety of initiatives – encompassing both enforcement and prevention-oriented work – in combination. In all cases, graduated enforcement strategies culminating in the deployment of ASBOs were combined with a range of preventive measures, some funded through mainstream services and others through special initiatives. There were, nevertheless, some differences in emphasis and tactics deployed.

A brief account of the three neighbourhoods, and their ASB initiatives, is provided below. The names of the areas have been anonymised to protect the confidentiality of respondents. More details on these areas are provided in Appendix B.

Southcity

The Southcity neighbourhood is in inner-city London. It is a deprived area with relatively high levels of crime, which has attracted funding from various regeneration and development streams. Housing provision is largely in the form of local authority-owned estates. The population is ethnically mixed (26% from black and minority ethnic [BME] groups).

The borough in which Southcity is located is known for taking an enforcement-oriented approach to ASB. It is among the highest users of

ASBOs nationally, and was one of the first local authorities to trial the new dispersal powers in 2004. By June 2004, over 80 ASBOs had been issued in the borough, of which only two were within the Southcity neighbourhood. The borough has an acute drugs problem, and ASBOs have been used to tackle this: by April 2004, 60% of its ASBOs related to drug users or dealers, of which only 3% were for borough residents.

Notwithstanding the borough's reputation for enforcement, there was ample evidence in the Southcity neighbourhood of preventive and community-oriented work on ASB. Relevant work includes projects being carried out as part of the local Neighbourhood Management Pathfinder,[6] the introduction of a safer neighbourhoods policing team, the activities of the Youth Inclusion Support Panel, and a variety of environmental initiatives.

Westerncity[7]

Westerncity is located in the outer suburbs of a city in South Wales. It is a deprived area that has had high levels of unemployment over the past few decades. Most housing provision is in the form of low-rise council housing estates. The population is very predominantly white. During the 1990s, joyriding and related ASB was a particularly severe problem in Westerncity. Cars were frequently burnt out in a neighbouring beauty spot. Over the past few years the car crime problem has diminished, although residents remain concerned about other forms of ASB associated with young people.

The local CDRP has tended to favour preventive over enforcement work on ASB. It has adopted a graduated response to ASB, with ASBOs used as the last resort. By mid-2004, only three ASBOs had been issued across the whole city, and none in the Westerncity neighbourhood. Other work in Westerncity that is relevant to ASB includes the Joseph Rowntree Foundation Communities that Care programme;[8] the Communities First project (a community engagement and regeneration programme funded by the Welsh Assembly); a local 'community house' established by a resident; regeneration of housing; and two early intervention programmes.

Midcity

Midcity is located in the outer suburbs of an East Midlands city. Like Westerncity, the neighbourhood comprises deprived edge-of-city council estates with some private provision. Fifteen per cent of the population are from BME groups. The area has had serious joyriding and associated youth ASB problems over the past 10 years – problems that persist today. Drug use and dealing is a growing problem in the area; a related concern over recent years has been the increase in gun crime across the city. There have been some incidents of gun crime in the Midcity area.

The local CDRP is becoming increasingly enforcement-oriented in its responses to ASB. In 2003/04, 10 ASBOs were issued across the city (excluding post-conviction ASBOs). In the Midcity area, five stand-alone ASBOs have been issued over the past five years, along with a number of post-conviction ASBOs. At the time of writing, around 20 individuals were under consideration for ASBOs in Midcity. As in Westerncity and Southcity, a range of other activities related to ASB are ongoing in Midcity. These include the work of the Area Team and Community Safety Panel, which aims to improve the health, well-being and education of Midcity residents; the city-wide 'Respect' campaign, which focuses on ASB in neighbourhoods and particularly prostitution and begging; the activities of the dedicated 'ASB task force' housing teams; and a variety of initiatives involving work with young people, children and parents.

Outline of the report

The remainder of this report is divided into five chapters. In Chapter 2, we look at the findings of our Office for National Statistics (ONS) survey and the British Crime Survey (BCS), in order to explore attitudes towards ASB among the general public. In Chapters 3 to 5, the focus of the report narrows to the three case-study neighbourhoods. Chapter 3 discusses the problems and impact of

---

6 See ODPM (2004).

7 This report draws on empirical material we gathered in Westerncity as part of an earlier study on ASB (see Jacobson et al, forthcoming), in addition to the material gathered specifically for this study.

8 See France and Crow (2001); Fairnington (2004).

ASB in the neighbourhoods, from the perspectives of the focus group participants and interviewees. Chapter 4 looks at our respondents' explanations for ASB, in terms of three 'narratives' that were frequently articulated. In Chapter 5, we consider how local responses to ASB emerge out of these contrasting explanations for the problem. Finally, Chapter 6 concludes the report with a discussion of the implications of our findings for strategic thinking on ASB. Our focus here is on identifying principles to assist the analysis of ASB problems, the search for solutions, and the management of ASB work. We also consider lessons to be learnt from this study for the government's handling of public opinion on ASB.

2

Views on ASB: the national picture

This chapter explores the general public's perceptions of ASB. It presents findings from our Office for National Statistics (ONS) survey, and also draws on the British Crime Survey (BCS). We aim to describe how people understand ASB and what impact it has on their lives. In particular the chapter discusses people's views on:

- what constitutes ASB;
- the impact of ASB on their daily lives;
- causes of youth ASB; and
- how to tackle ASB.

What is ASB?

We wanted to find out what issues people think are included in the government's ASB strategy. Half of respondents were asked an open-ended question, and half were asked to select items from a checklist. The checklist included problems included in the Home Office ASB typology and others not usually thought of as ASB (see Table 1).

Respondents clearly associated the government's approach to ASB with problems of disorder, specifically related to young people. For both

Table 1: What do you think the government means by anti-social behaviour?

	Free responses[a] (*n*=831)	%		Responses to checklist[b] (*n*=847)	%
1.	Vandalism/graffiti/hooligans	17	1.	Rowdy teenagers on the streets/ youths hanging around	71
2.	Youths hanging around/people being a nuisance	16	2.	Drug dealing	63
3.	Drinking, drunk and disorderly	15	3.	Noisy neighbours	44
4.	Unacceptable/bad behaviour; rowdyism; bad language	13	4.	Mugging	44
			5.	Burglary	42
5.	Crime: muggings; burglary; criminal damage	12	6.	Graffiti	34
6.	Noisy neighbours	10	7.	Speeding	34
7.	Noise; traffic noise; pollution	8	8.	Traffic noise and pollution	22
8.	Violence; fighting	7	9.	None of these	2
9.	Intimidation; offensive/threatening/ aggressive behaviour; harassment	7	10.	Don't know	8
10.	Drug use; drug dealing	6			
11.	Yobbish behaviour/yob culture	4			
12.	Disruption/disturbance to community	2			
13.	Litter; fly-tipping	2			
14.	Speeding	1			
15.	Don't know	5			

Notes:

[a] Question: 'What do you think the government means by anti-social behaviour?'

[b] Question: 'Which of the problems on this card do you think the [government's] strategy is aiming to reduce?'

Figure 1: Worst forms of ASB in your local area (*n*=1,682)

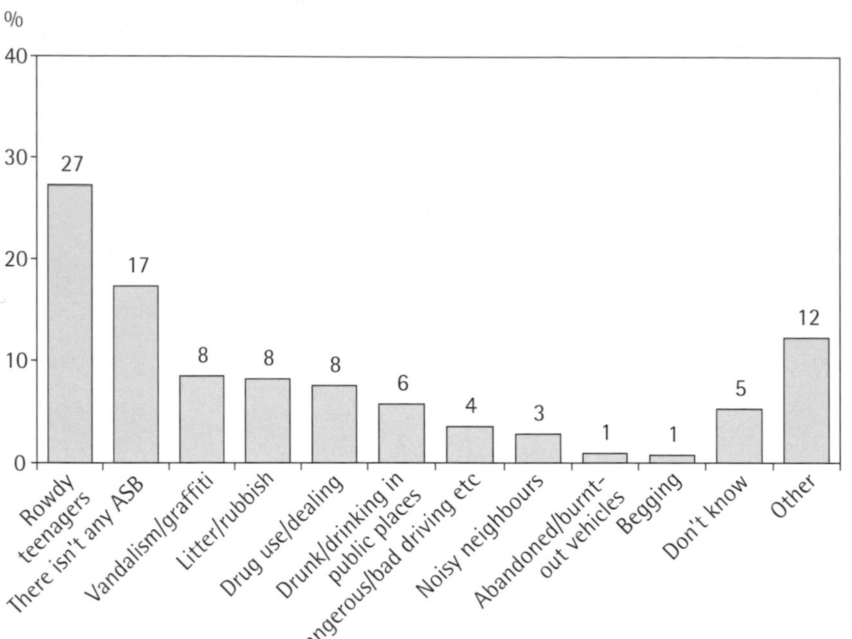

groups of respondents, rowdy teenagers on the street came high on the list of ASB issues. However, two thirds of those selecting items from the checklist thought that the government strategy placed an emphasis on mugging or burglary, and a fifth included traffic noise and pollution – issues that are not part of the national focus. It seems, therefore, that many think the government's strategy is even broader than it currently is.

Only 6% of those respondents asked for a free response mentioned drug use or dealing – suggesting that such problems are not at the forefront of most people's thoughts. However, 63% of respondents choosing from the checklist cited drug dealing as an issue targeted by the government's ASB strategy. By contrast, problems associated with drink were more commonly cited in the free response – by 15% of people.

ASB in the local area

Our ONS respondents were asked what was the worst form of ASB in their local area. No prompt was used for this question, but over a quarter (27%) came up with the same answer: rowdy teenagers on the street/youths hanging about (see Figure 1). The BCS also points to relatively high levels of concern about 'teenagers hanging around'. When asked in the 2002/03 BCS about the biggest ASB problem in the respondents' area, this was the most common response, again selected by a quarter of respondents (Thorpe and Wood, 2004). In the 2003/04 BCS, speeding traffic was included in the list of problems. This option displaced teenagers by a small margin: 19% cited traffic and 17% teenagers (Wood, 2004).[9] Since 1992, 'teenagers hanging around' has also consistently been within the top three ASB problems described by BCS respondents as 'big or fairly big' local problems.[10]

While environmental crime attracted some concern, more than one in six respondents said there was no ASB where they lived. Logistic regression was carried out on the top five responses to determine the key predictors of 'worst ASB' type (for full results see Appendix C). We found that younger respondents were more likely than their elders to cite 'rowdy teenagers' as the worst local ASB problem: with, for example, 32% of those aged 16 to 24 seeing this as the worst problem, compared with 18% of

[9] The issue of 'speeding traffic' had not been included in previous surveys. In the 2003/04 BCS, although second to the problem of speeding, 'teenagers hanging around' was still a long way ahead of the next 'biggest problem': drug use and dealing, cited by 9% (Wood, 2004).

[10] In the 2003/04 BCS, 29% of respondents cited rubbish or litter as a fairly/very big problem; 28% vandalism and graffiti; and 27% teenagers hanging around (Wood 2004).

Table 2: Effects of ASB issues on quality of life (%)

n=1,682	Don't know/doesn't occur/ no effect	Occurs, and *minor* effect	Occurs and *fairly/ very big* effect	Effect (all levels)
Rowdy teenagers in the street	49	32	19	51
Drug use/dealing	65	17	17	34
Vandalism/graffiti	46	38	17	55
Litter/rubbish	42	41	17	58
Abandoned/burnt-out vehicles	73	19	10	29
Noisy neighbours	76	15	9	24
Begging	88	7	6	13

Note: Percentages may not add up to 100% due to rounding.

those aged 65 to 74.[11] One explanation for this might be that younger people are more likely than older people to be victims of crime and ASB committed by other young people, and are therefore more aware of it. Respondents over retirement age were less likely than others to say there were ASB problems in their area; and those who did were more likely to cite litter and graffiti as the worst problem.

Other predictors of 'worst' problems include educational achievement and ethnicity. Graduates were less likely than others to cite drug use and dealing as the worst form of ASB where they lived – perhaps because they tend to live in areas with fewer drug problems – and more likely to cite litter and rubbish. Younger respondents and respondents from BME groups were the most likely to consider drug use and dealing to be the worst form of ASB in their area. Again, these findings may reflect their greater exposure to problems associated with drug use.

The impact of ASB

BCS figures suggest that public concern about ASB grew in the second half of the 1990s (as crime fell), but then plateaued between 2000 and 2002/03 and then fell slightly. For instance, the percentage of respondents saying ASB was a fairly or very big problem in their area was 21% in 2002/03, but only 16% in 2003/04[12] (Finney and Toofail, 2004, p 19). These figures indicate that, for a majority of people across England and Wales, ASB is not a major concern. For a minority of people, however, ASB clearly is a significant issue. Moreover, surveys show that serious problems of ASB tend to be concentrated in certain types of neighbourhoods.

According to the 2003/04 BCS, those in inner-city areas (34%) and 'hard-pressed'[13] areas (31%) were significantly more likely than others to perceive high levels of ASB (Wood, 2004, p 15). (The average for England and Wales was 16%.) Twenty-five per cent of Londoners perceived the levels of disorder in their area to be 'high', but within London there was a marked inner–outer split, with perceptions of higher levels of disorder among inner-city Londoners (Moore and Yeo, 2004).

Other research suggests that high levels of perceived ASB are associated with dissatisfaction with one's neighbourhood. The 2002 London Household Survey[14] (see Millie et al, forthcoming) revealed that Londoners who are

[11] A similar finding emerged from the 2003/04 BCS, which found that 22% of those aged 16 to 24 cited teenagers hanging around as the biggest problem, compared with 13% of 65 to 74 year-olds and 8% of those aged 75 and over (Wood, 2004).

[12] These figures are derived from responses to questions about seven individual ASB issues: abandoned or burnt-out cars; noisy neighbours or loud parties; people being drunk or rowdy in public places; people using or dealing drugs; teenagers hanging around on the streets; rubbish or litter lying around; and vandalism, graffiti and other deliberate damage to property.

[13] Based on the ACORN classification of residential neighbourhoods.

[14] The 2002 London Household Survey was conducted for the Greater London Authority, with a sample of 8,000 households.

fairly or very dissatisfied with their neighbourhoods also have serious concerns about ASB and crime in general. For example, of respondents who were very dissatisfied with their neighbourhood, 64% also thought that vandalism and hooliganism were a serious problem, compared with 13% of those who were very satisfied. Similarly, 41% of the 'very dissatisfied' saw troublesome teenagers/children as a problem, compared with only 4% of the 'very satisfied'.

Effects of ASB issues on quality of life

In the ONS survey, respondents were asked how much their quality of life was affected by different ASB issues. Unlike the question on 'worst ASB problem', responses were given to a set list of concerns. Table 2 shows that quality of life for most people is not greatly affected by ASB. Mirroring responses to the BCS question of 'worst problem where you live', 'rowdy teenagers' was the ASB issue that most frequently had a fairly or very big effect on quality of life. This was closely followed by drug use/dealing, vandalism/graffiti and litter/rubbish. If 'minor effect' responses are included, the issue most frequently said to impact on quality of life was litter/rubbish (58%). However, while litter and graffiti are pervasive, we might surmise that they are rarely seriously intrusive on most people's lives, as this is not an issue people raise in local discussions.

Again, logistic regression was used to find predictors of impact on quality of life (see Appendix C). As with the 'worst form of ASB' analysis, people of retirement age were less likely than others to be affected by rowdy teenagers. Conversely, being aged 30 or under was a predictor that rowdy teenagers affected your life. Other predictors were lack of formal qualifications, renting from the local authority/housing association, living in London and being from a BME background. For drug use/dealing, predictors of effect were being from a BME background, renting from the local authority/housing association, and having no formal qualifications.

The 2003/04 BCS explored the impact of ASB by asking whether any of 16 behaviours had a 'bad effect' on respondents' lives. Approaching two thirds (61%) reported no bad effects from these types of ASB. The issues cited most often were speeding traffic and teenagers hanging around (both mentioned by 11% of people). The BCS also found that respondents living in 'hard-pressed' areas were more likely than others to report that young people hanging around had a high impact on their quality of life (Wood, 2004).

Perceived causes of youth ASB

Our ONS survey asked about people's perceptions of the causes of youth ASB, picking up on this key area of concern. Respondents

Figure 2: Which of these do you think are the three main causes of youth ASB? (*n*=1,682)

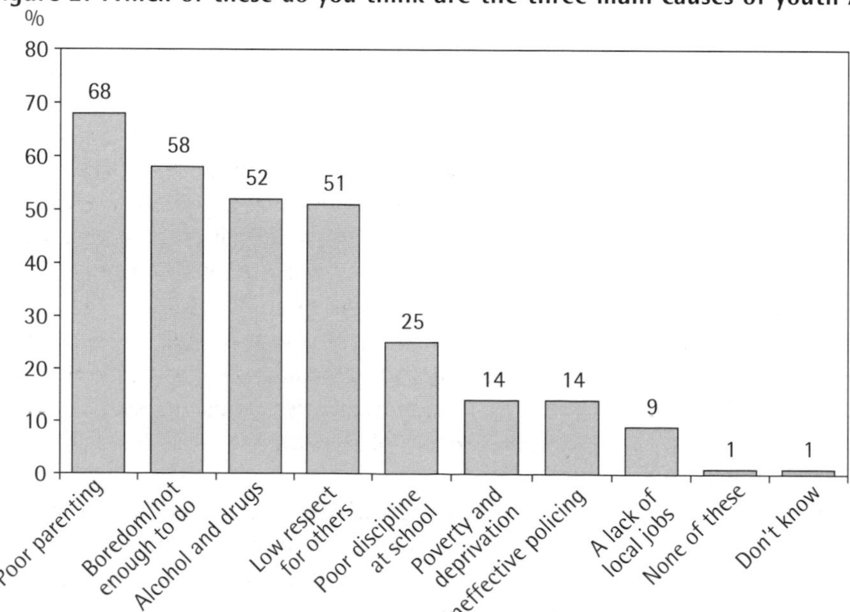

Note: Percentages do not add up to 100 as this question is multi-coded.

were asked what they perceived to be the three most significant causes from a list of options. Figure 2 shows that people tend to link youth ASB to broader cultural or social problems – with 'poor parenting', 'alcohol and drugs' and 'low respect for others' cited by 68%, 52% and 51% respectively. Another major cause of youthful ASB was thought to be boredom and not enough to do (cited by 58% of respondents).

Ineffective policing, poverty and unemployment were given little weight by respondents. This suggests that the argument we developed in the previous chapter, about the relevance of social policy and economic issues (alongside cultural issues) to the emergence of ASB as a priority, is unlikely to have much resonance among the general public. However, concepts such as 'poor parenting' and 'alcohol and drugs' are very broad. Respondents who cite these as causes of youth ASB may have a wide range of views on how and why these factors contribute to the problem.

How to tackle ASB

Our ONS survey also looked at views on tackling ASB. Respondents were asked: 'If there was more money to spend in your local area on tackling ASB, should this be spent on tough action against perpetrators, or preventive action to deal with the causes?' This hypothetical – and arguably loaded – question was designed to get a feel for the extent to which the enforcement-oriented tone of the government's TOGETHER campaign reflects public attitudes. Only 20% of respondents chose tough action against perpetrators as the best strategy for tackling local ASB, compared with 66% who opted for preventive action (some of whom might have wanted to avoid appearing too harsh to the interviewer) and 11% who said both.

Men were more likely to support tough action than women, and those over retirement age were more likely to do so than younger people (see Appendix C). Better-educated people and house owners were less likely to do so, while Londoners were more tough-minded than others, which might reflect the fact that concern about ASB tends to be higher in London than elsewhere.

Around two thirds of the respondents (63%) had heard of ASBOs as a method of tackling ASB. All respondents had the order explained to them, and were then asked their views on its likely effectiveness. Answers to this question revealed considerable support for ASBOs, with 60% saying they would be quite or very effective in dealing with disruptive neighbours, and 55% quite or fairly effective in targeting youths who disrupt their neighbourhood.

Our ONS survey asked if the police or local authority should do more to tackle ASB. Unsurprisingly (given that when people are asked whether more should be done about any given problem, most say 'yes'), a majority of respondents did feel that both the police and local authority should do more. It is interesting, however, that this was not a large majority, with around a third saying these agencies should do a lot more, and around a quarter saying that they should do a little more.

Views on ASB: from the national to the local picture

The findings of the survey research presented here indicate that for a majority of people in England and Wales, ASB is not a big problem. On the other hand, it is an acute concern for *a sizeable minority* of people in *some* areas; these areas are most likely to be urban and deprived, and problems of ASB may be closely interlinked with other problems, such as crime and fear of crime.

Anti-social behaviour can take a great many forms. Of all ASB problems, it is youth ASB (described in terms of young people hanging around, or rowdy young people) that appears to be the most visible and worrisome. Interestingly, youth ASB tends to be more of a concern to younger rather than older people. In contrast to problems relating to young people, certain other ASB issues, such as vandalism or litter and rubbish, may have a wider but less serious impact on people's lives.

Survey findings such as those reported in this chapter provide a useful insight into levels of concern about ASB and general perceptions of the problem. However, because of the great variety in manifestations and experiences of ASB, there are limitations to what we can learn from surveys about how ASB affects the day-to-day lives of individuals. Even if we consider specific forms of ASB, such as 'rowdy young people' or 'vandalism', we should recognise that these problems can take very different forms and cause very different reactions in different social contexts.

In particular, certain forms of ASB in deprived neighbourhoods may be worse, in qualitative as well as quantitative terms, than their equivalents in more prosperous neighbourhoods. On the other hand, tolerance for some kinds of ASB may be lower in relatively well-off areas. In the next three chapters, we turn to the findings of our research in three deprived neighbourhoods. We examine how ASB impacts on residents' lives, how residents and professionals understand ASB, and the potential responses to these problems.

3

Problems and impact of ASB in the case-study areas

Our three case-study neighbourhoods were partly selected on the grounds that they all had features – such as relatively high crime levels and high levels of deprivation – that are commonly associated with problems of ASB (see Chapter 1). The findings of the interviews and focus group discussions confirmed that ASB is indeed a significant feature of daily life in these neighbourhoods.

In all three neighbourhoods the following four key ASB themes emerged in the interviews and focus groups (each of which will be considered in detail below):

- misbehaving children and young people;
- problems associated with misuse of drugs and, to a lesser degree, alcohol;
- neighbour disputes and 'problem families'; and
- a pervasive sense of powerlessness associated with all these problems.

Misbehaving children and young people

Supporting the ONS and BCS findings, respondents (both residents and agency representatives) spoke much more frequently about ASB problems associated with children and young people than about any other kind of problem. More specifically, their key concerns were:

- boisterous and rowdy behaviour by children;
- young people congregating in groups;
- young people causing damage to property and the environment; and
- anti-social use of cars and motorbikes by children and young people.

Rowdy behaviour by children was a source of concern to many respondents – who also often talked about children being out on the streets late at night. Rowdiness concerned people not only because of the noise and general disturbance caused, but also because it produced a (possibly exaggerated) sense of general disorder:

> The main complaints I get from local residents a lot of the time is kids playing on the street and causing annoyance, and when the kids are confronted they often turn around and break windows and shout abuse. (Midcity police sergeant)

It was frequently stressed that young people congregating in groups was intimidating – whether or not the groups were doing anything harmful. As noted by a local councillor in Midcity: 'You get youths congregating and often I have to say it is not sinister at all; but the elderly see it as a threat'. A community activist from Westerncity observed:

> The evenings are the worst because, if they're outside your door and you're trying to do something, even if it's watching television, and there's noise outside. It's not a life, is it, when you're continually pestered.

Even where young people's behaviour is not intentionally threatening, their apparent lack of consideration for others can add to the annoyance. Participants in the young people's focus group in Midcity, talking with obvious bravado, showed little concern for how their behaviour might impact on older people:

I[15] Do you understand why old people get upset about young people hanging around on the streets and so on?
R1 No – it depends on what comes out of your mouth at the time.
I What could be done to try and sort that situation out?
R2 Give them ear plugs or something.

Frequent complaints were made about children and young people causing destruction – through arson, graffiti, general vandalism, throwing stones at houses or passing cars. For example:

> There were the decent kids that ran the sports centre, but [others] burnt it down. Something is in their system. (Midcity retired people's focus group)

In Westerncity, various respondents identified a particular problem with primary-school-aged children: 'They're the ones going round lighting fires outside flats. You know, they're regenerating [the flats], and then they go and melt all the PVC' (community activist). Similarly, a participant in the retired people's focus group observed:

> Sunday night around the back of the school, there was about six children, ranging from seven to 11, throwing stones at the school with all their might.

The anti-social use of cars, motorbikes and scooters by children and young people was also considered a problem in all three neighbourhoods. There were complaints about young people riding motorbikes or mopeds on pavements or in public parks: for example, a participant in the Southcity young women's focus group commented: 'It's like one o'clock in the morning and they're just zooming up and down.... It's a problem for everybody'. Some respondents also talked about problems with motorised miniature scooters.

Concerns about joyriding and car crime in general were particularly evident in Westerncity and Midcity.[16] Although much of this activity involves serious criminal offences (such as car theft), residents also have to suffer the anti-social consequences:

> My nephew, if there are loads of joyriders he's like, "I don't like it, I don't like it", and he puts his hands over his ears. (Midcity parents' focus group)

> I went there last week and my mother was very ill in bed, and there was someone going up and down the pavement on their motorbike, and I said: "Do you mind not doing that, my mother really isn't very well". And I looked and his eyes were out of his head, he followed me all the way down the road: "What's it to you? I hate people like you!", following me all the way down the road shouting at me. ([Midcity retired people's focus group)

Drug and alcohol misuse

Problems associated with the use and dealing of illegal drugs were often cited as ASB, most commonly in Southcity, but also in the other two neighbourhoods. In all three places, cannabis use by adolescents was said to be common and Class A drug use by young adults was said to be increasing. Drug use and dealing was associated with ASB for various reasons. Concerns centred on:

- young people congregating in groups – cannabis smoking often being a group activity;
- the fears provoked by visible drug use and the unpredictable and offensive behaviour associated with drug consumption;
- the impact on children who come across drug misuse in public places;
- broader violence and disorder linked to drug dealing or binge drinking.

In Southcity, several respondents talked about groups of youths who sat around outside a community centre and smoked cannabis, making others feel nervous about going in and out of the centre. Some respondents also spoke about the unpredictable, offensive or disturbing behaviour associated with Class A drug use:

> Now, if they want to take drugs and kill themselves, feel free. My objection is: get

[15] 'I' refers to the interviewer; 'R' refers to respondents.

[16] Car crime, and particularly joyriding, have long been associated with the Westerncity neighbourhood. These problems have reduced over the past five years, but there are fears they may currently be on the rise again. In Midcity, these are very much current concerns.

> it out of my face. I do not want to see dickheads ... with needles, and they're dirty needles. And the usual thing is when they've smoked their crack, and they either piss, shit or vomit – and it's usually outside of somebody's door in a stairwell. Why should we have to continually put up with this? (Southcity community activist)

Other respondents spoke of visible drug use being, in itself, frightening or upsetting:

R1 The worst thing I've seen is somebody injecting themselves when I was walking down the street with my little girl. I was disgusted, I screamed at the fella....

R2 I live opposite the park and my daughter was on the balcony and she saw it – she is only nine.

R1 My little girl's seven, she was petrified: "Don't stick that in me". (Southcity parents' focus group)

There were also worries about children picking up drug paraphernalia; and some respondents voiced concerns about children acting as 'runners' for drug dealers. Another issue raised was potential violence and disorder associated specifically with drug dealing. For example, a local councillor in Midcity told of a family that 'peddle in drugs and live in a quiet part of the city'. The effect this had on the neighbourhood was that 'people live in pure hell with youngsters queuing up in the middle of the night for drugs'. At the most serious end of the spectrum, some in Midcity talked about a rise in gun crime related to drug dealing:

> There have been shootings in [Midcity] definitely; it is on the increase there. I really do believe it's down to (a) the culture is more widespread; (b) the thing about finding new drug markets, or taking over existing markets.... The guns are just so freely available. (Midcity ASB coordinator)

ASB related to alcohol was also discussed in the three neighbourhoods, although this was mentioned less often than drug-related ASB – possibly because drink-related ASB tends to be associated more with town centres than residential neighbourhoods. Respondents spoke about young people congregating to drink, and the trouble that results – for example: 'Anti-social behaviour normally proves worse on the weekends when they start drinking from off-licences and hanging around. We've had instances of people throwing bottles at buses' (Westerncity community activist). In Midcity, some spoke about groups of up to 30 young people drinking outside shopping centres; and here, under-age drinking was a particular concern. In Westerncity, a project worker commented that although there was a perception that drug misuse was a more serious local issue, the problems associated with alcohol – in particular, under-age drinking and binge drinking (by people of all ages) – were greater.

Neighbour disputes and 'problem families'

Anti-social behaviour that takes the form of neighbour disputes was sometimes, but not frequently, discussed by our respondents. It was made clear that when these problems do occur, their impact can be very severe. Hence it appears that while ASB problems relating to substance misuse and young people tend to be more diffuse, neighbour-related ASB problems can have a more serious impact on a smaller number of people.

A community activist in Southcity talked about a family who lived in the neighbouring flat and attracted large groups of young people who would sit in their shared hallway and drink, smoke cannabis, spit, urinate and vomit. He complained also that the family had a large dog, which they kept on a balcony adjoining his own. This prevented his children from using their balcony because they were scared of the dog and, moreover, the dog mess went all over their own balcony when it rained.

Neighbour disputes can cause fear and intimidation – the impact of which can be all the more severe because the victims feel scared in their own homes:

> I've been threatened if his dogs get over into my garden he won't be responsible for them ... I've got three babies! I don't want dogs barking all night and day, but I haven't opened my mouth in the last

> three weeks. (Westerncity community activist)

> I had a neighbour for one year and she tormented me morning, noon and night; I never slept. (Southcity retired person)

A related issue that occasionally emerged in the interviews and focus groups was that of the 'problem family'. Problem families were described as large and chaotic, and engaged in criminal as well as anti-social behaviour that could impact on a whole street or neighbourhood and not just the immediate neighbours. In Midcity, a community development worker talked about families comprising up to 60 individuals in total, which were 'interlinked with each other in a sort of clannish nature'. Also in Midcity, a community regeneration worker talked of a family who had recently moved into the area and would 'come out at night and cause mayhem – motorbikes, drinking, lobbing drinking cans at some people's houses'.

A sense of powerlessness

From much of what was said about local problems, it was clear that incidents of ASB can provoke a profound sense of powerlessness in the victims: that is, the sense that these incidents epitomise the lack of control that local residents have over their social environment. Hence, this sense of powerlessness is not only a consequence of, but also an integral element of, experiences of ASB. One result of this is a vicious circle, whereby ASB provokes a sense of powerlessness, which can in itself make ASB more able to flourish as it goes on unchecked.

One aspect of this sense of powerlessness is the fear of retaliation that prevents victims from trying to stop disorderly, offensive or disturbing behaviour. A local councillor in Midcity commented that if a resident decides to become a witness – for example for an ASBO application – then intimidation can be at a 'frightening' level. Various respondents complained about the abuse experienced by residents who attempt to intervene:

> As soon as someone comes out of the house to speak to them, they get verbal abuse and stones thrown at the windows. (Midcity police constable)

> My son told me that if I shout at them I will only end up getting a brick through the window, and that's true. (Midcity retired people's focus group)

> You can't say anything to them, you get abuse; in fact, they know more of the law better than the police, so what can you do? And if you say something to them they probably say something to their mother and father and the next thing they are knocking at your door. (Westerncity retired people's focus group)

A community activist in Southcity said that in his 'own country' – Somalia – he would not accept the levels of bad behaviour he encounters in Britain; but here he has to accept that he can't do anything: 'People have scared me many times ... I have to put my face down. I have to not respond when they're knocking on my windows'.

Many respondents commented that young people are largely immune to admonishment – thanks to their general lack of respect for authority:

> Today you can't tell them not to do certain things: it's a case of, "Who are you?". And half the time they just look at you daft and just carry on doing what they were doing anyway. (Westerncity community activist)

> There was a boy out there the other day throwing stones at my CCTV camera, and I bet he was no older than eight or nine; and I said, "Would you stop that please," and he said, "What are you going to do?". And clearly there was nothing I could do and he knew that. (Midcity project worker)

> Youngsters today are almost prepared to take you on. They know their rights far more than we did. (Midcity local councillor)

The difficulty of confronting young people was attributed also to the lack of 'community':

> I think a lot of residents feel disempowered because they don't have the in-depth community knowledge of the people on the street. They don't know the young people concerned and the remedy of, 'I will see your father or mother'. (Westerncity police constable)

A Westerncity community activist recalled the time when locals would challenge youngsters who misbehaved; but today, he said, people are too frightened to do so. As a result, 'A lot of people shut the door and think the problem will go away. But it doesn't.'

Our focus group participants frequently complained about the pointlessness of calling the police or other agencies when there are incidents of ASB – because the agencies are not interested, or do not care, or do not have the necessary resources for a timely response. A participant in the Midcity parents' group talked about the failure of the police to respond when her daughter was attacked:

> That lad had my daughter on the floor … I phoned the police and they didn't come out. Then the second time I reported it, it took them about two hours to come out. They went over to see him and they didn't do anything about it.

Some respondents commented that even if the police or other agencies *want* to take action against ASB, they cannot do so because their hands are tied:

R1 You daren't say anything to them; you tell the police but the police say it's not a priority.
R2 The police are not allowed to box their ears or anything….
R3 We've got wardens that don't do anything – they have no authority…. (Midcity retired people's focus group)

Comments by the young people in our focus groups reinforce the picture of a younger generation that feels willing and able to challenge the authority of the police and other agencies. Their particular scorn for wardens and Police Community Support Officers (PCSOs) was evident:

R1 Wardens, they stop us.
R2 … Twats, they are like coppers but worse. They are like coppers but they are not official coppers.
I What do the rest of you think of the wardens?
[General swearing]
R3 They just walk around and arrest people, following them wherever they go. (Midcity young people's focus group)

R1 … I was walking down and they [PCSOs] stopped me and asked if I was old enough to be smoking a cigarette. I just looked at him, grabbed the cigarette and laughed … I just don't see the point.
R2 They're just a joke.
R1 They're like security guards, yeah.
R3 Some of the boys round here call them fake police; they think they're toy police. (Southcity young men's focus group)

Two youth workers in Southcity were firmly of the belief that young people have little respect for officers such as PCSOs: 'The value of [PCSOs] is that pensioners, wrongly, are comforted by the sight of a man in uniform.… But in terms of frightening the young people out of anti-social behaviour – [laughs]!'. Other agency representatives, however, were more optimistic about the capacity of local officers to engage with young people; for example, a Westerncity PCSO said that he and his colleagues had managed to build positive relationships with local children – which had had a beneficial impact on youth nuisance. Nonetheless, he also complained that:

> You walk along the street and they lift your jacket and they go, "Where's your handcuff? What can you do to me, like? What are you going to do?" … And they're like, "What can you arrest me for – public order?". And they'll read out what the definition of public order is – you know, that's unbelievable.

Local concerns and national implications

Our findings suggest that in neighbourhoods in which levels of ASB are relatively high, issues relating to youth and children tend to cause particular concern. Other key concerns relate to drug and alcohol misuse, and the impact of neighbour disputes and 'problem families'.

One of the most insidious consequences of local problems of ASB can be the sense of powerlessness among those who experience it. National policy on ASB has sought to address this sense of powerlessness – and replace it with a conviction, on the part of the general public, that ASB can and will be successfully tackled. However, to understand the potential for success of the national campaign, we need some insight into how the public and professionals understand ASB: that is, their views on the causes of ASB and what should be done about it. These issues are dealt with in the two chapters that follow.

4

Explaining ASB: local narratives

Respondents in the case-study neighbourhoods were asked their views on the causes of ASB. We found that their explanations for ASB tended to be rooted in broader conceptions of social and cultural change, and that three main strands of thought, or 'narratives of ASB', emerged in what was said:

1. **Social and moral decline**: Problems of ASB are symptoms of wider social and cultural change – more specifically, a decline in moral standards and family values.
2. **Disengaged youth and families**: Problems of ASB are rooted in the increasing disengagement from wider society of a significant minority of children and young people and (in many cases) their families.
3. **'Kids will be kids'**: Problems of ASB largely reflect the age-old tendency for young people to get into trouble, challenge boundaries and antagonise their elders.

The above narratives are not mutually exclusive or discrete: most respondents tended to combine elements of each in talking about ASB. In essence, however, they are alternative viewpoints, and hence can be seen as three 'ideal types' of explanation for ASB.

Unsurprisingly, since respondents spoke mostly about ASB committed by children and young people when asked about local problems, the three narratives are largely focused on youth ASB – although the narrative of social and moral decline is somewhat broader in scope.

The first two narratives assume that problems of ASB are getting worse: because of a generalised process of decline; or because of the increasing disengagement of a minority of British youth and/or their families. The third narrative does not assume that problems of ASB are necessarily getting worse in themselves; but suggests that *concern about* ASB is becoming more prominent.

To some extent, the narratives play out tensions between younger and older generations – the older generation are more likely to articulate the first (and possibly the second) narrative, and the younger generation to suggest the third. In contrast, ASB practitioners with social welfare and support roles tend to favour the second narrative and to a lesser extent the third.

Social and moral decline

The narrative of decline was most frequently articulated by participants in the retired people's focus groups in all three neighbourhoods, and to a lesser extent by some of the parents and community activists who participated in the research. This viewpoint emerged much more rarely in interviews with professionals, and was based on various ideas:

- In the past, the population as a whole was much more civil.
- Young people are becoming increasingly disrespectful.
- Government and other institutions show a lack of moral leadership.

Ideas about decline were often founded on nostalgic conceptions of a better past:

R1 I am sorry to say but I think we've seen the best of this country.
R2 And we won't see it again.
R1 I have told my girls to go to New Zealand and make a good life out there.
R3 It's an English way of life as it used to be.
(Midcity retired people's focus group)

> I think the worst thing I ever did [as a child] was pinch apples. And we thought we were really doing something wicked, and we dared not go home and tell our family. (Westerncity retired people's focus group)

The general decline in behavioural standards was thought to be manifest in ASB committed by young people and evident in their lack of respect or sense of responsibility for others. (It is interesting to recall that 51% of respondents in our ONS survey cited 'low respect for others' as a cause of youth ASB.) The following exchange occurred in the Southcity parents' focus group:

R1 How many times do you see someone get up at the bus stop for a lady to sit or an old person? The number of times you see them there with the trainers up on the back of the seat in front – you get a mouthful.
R2 There are lots of adults that won't stand up now.
R3 I was brought up properly so I always do, but it doesn't seem to be as common as it used to. If I was on the bus with my mum and I didn't give up my seat for an adult I would get a clip around the ear.

Similar concerns were raised by a Westerncity youth project coordinator:

> Things like respect and discipline all seem to have gone out of the window. I know people say it's all old fashioned, but I don't think so because I think it's the very essence of being able to live with others and integrate with others.

From the 'decline' perspective, part of the blame for current problems was thought to rest with parents who fail to pass on positive social and moral values. Doubtless a significant proportion of the 68% of our ONS respondents who said 'poor parenting' was a cause of ASB held to this kind of viewpoint.[17] The culpability of parents was stressed in the following comments:

> If the parents don't have any values to pass on to their children, then they grow up and pass on the same sort of non-values to their offspring again and it becomes a cycle. (Westerncity youth project manager)

> They have to have some lead, whether it's the parents or teachers, they have to have someone showing them right and wrong. (Southcity parents' focus group)

R1 Don't forget that discipline starts at home and that's where it's all gone wrong – it starts with the parents....
R2 ... To be quite blunt about it, morons breed morons – that's my opinion. (Midcity retired people's focus group)

We have already seen – in the discussion of 'powerlessness' in the previous chapter – that many respondents complained of the impotence of statutory agencies with respect to ASB. For some, this problem betrays a lack of moral leadership in Britain. Successive governments, and institutions such as the courts, the police and schools, are accused of failing to instil discipline and morality in the British people. For example:

> The teachers at school can only do so much now, because it's a nanny state, and the kids are let off things because the teacher won't get involved in case they get sorted out. (Southcity retired people's focus group)

Similarly, in the equivalent group in Midcity there were complaints about: 'No police and no discipline – the government has took the discipline out of schools'; and about 'soft' sentencing and the weakness of the criminal justice system as a whole. There is a need for change, it was argued; and this change has 'got to start with the Law Lords'.

Disengaged youth and families

A different kind of explanation for ASB is that the problems largely stem from the fact that a sizeable minority of British youth are increasingly disengaged or alienated from wider society and sometimes their own families. This disengagement is thought to be manifest in behaviour that is senseless, inconsiderate or

[17] We shall see below, in the discussion of the 'disengaged youth' perspective, that some respondents had a somewhat different view of how parenting problems contribute to ASB. Hence, it should be recognised that not all the 68% of respondents who cited 'poor parenting' as a cause of ASB would have had the same understanding of the term.

malicious – because the young people do not have the ability or the will to behave in other ways.[18] There are clear overlaps with the 'decline' perspective in that the latter also emphasises an apparent lack of values among young people. But the essential difference is that the 'decline' narrative sees the root of ASB problems lying in the moral decay of society at large; whereas the 'disengagement' narrative traces the problems back to disadvantage – social, cultural and economic – within particular families and communities.

This 'disengagement' narrative emerged most frequently in interviews with professionals in the three neighbourhoods – especially those working with children and young people. Some of the residents who were interviewed or participated in the focus groups also spoke in these terms. The issues of parenting problems and low aspirations are often at the centre of explanations offered here. The following two quotations sum up the concerns:

> There are a number of youths who are definitely disillusioned, disaffected with society as a whole; some of them have low educational attainment; some of them have disengaged themselves from everything. (Westerncity headmaster)

> They have no stability; they have no rights and wrongs; they have no social rules. They have no – very little – social skills. It's obviously chaotic, no respect for the people living around here. (Westerncity youth worker)

Parenting problems are often seen as an important contributory factor to the problem of 'disengaged youth'. The concern here, however, is not so much with the perceived moral failings of parents, as in the 'decline' narrative. Rather, the focus is on parents' inability – stemming from their own poor experiences of being parented, or from the social or personal circumstances in which they find themselves – to interact constructively and positively with their children. Generally, therefore, this narrative reflects a more sympathetic approach to the perpetrators of ASB than the narrative of decline.

A youth worker in Southcity talked of the problems that arise when family breakdowns have occurred in successive generations, leading to 'a build-up of the negativity of struggling through' as parents. Various respondents talked about parents who fail to care properly for their children because of their own drug or alcohol problems, or because they became parents at a very young age:

> A lot of these kids ain't got homes, or the homes they've got ain't worth a toss. Either mum's a junkie or dad's a junkie, or mum or dad's an alcoholic. (Southcity community activist)

The result of ineffective parenting is said to be children and young people whose behaviour is uncontrolled and uncontrollable:

> If you've got seven-, eight-, nine-year-olds running around the streets at 10, 11 o'clock at night, that's not just the child's problem. The cause of that has got to be what's happening within the home. (Westerncity project coordinator)

> The problem we have got is that we don't enable young people to have the resources within themselves to cope.... It is about not having the support within the family and the parents. The result of that is that young people have no inner resources to do it themselves. (Midcity community development worker)

It was also argued that many children readily resort to violence and abuse in potential conflict situations because this is what they learn from parents who have 'a massive inability to deal with conflict' (Southcity youth worker). The same respondent also talked about parents not having the ability to set boundaries for their children, and the problems that result from this: 'A lot of kids just get what they want – so they come into the [youth] project with: "We want this; we want that"'. Similarly, a Westerncity youth worker commented: 'It seems to me more and more

[18] This viewpoint relates to another perspective not explicitly articulated in our case-study sites: that ASB is not simply a behavioural problem, but is often caused by learning disabilities or by psychological or psychiatric conditions such as Attention Deficit Hyperactivity Disorder, autistic spectrum disorders or depression. Work in this area is currently being carried out by the Antisocial Behaviour Interdisciplinary Research Group, at the Institute of Psychiatry, King's College London.

parents are buying more and more for their children, and not enough time is being spent with them'.

The young people in the Midcity focus group strongly rejected the notion that parenting problems might be a cause of ASB. When asked if poor parenting can be blamed for ASB, one participant retorted: 'No: how can it be your fucking parents – what the fuck do your parents do? They try and keep you out of trouble, not put you in it.'

Educational problems were also discussed by some who articulated the 'disengaged youth' narrative. Respondents pointed out that many young people involved in serious ASB are also truanting or excluded from school, or have left school with no qualifications. This and other factors can produce very low aspirations among young people. A community development worker in Midcity noted: 'A lot of young men, particularly the 12- to 13-year-olds, are beginning to say things like: "Well, I will just go out nicking 'cause I can get some money"'. The following exchange in Midcity young people's focus group illustrated the participants' low aspirations:

I Where do you all see yourselves in about five years' time?
R1 Down town sitting outside a shop, hat in front of you, bottle of cider at the side....
R2 I know where we'll be in a few years' time – on the dole. I don't think of the future.
R3 I don't want to be working all my life; I've got better things to do.

Some respondents spoke also about socioeconomic factors that play a part in limiting young people's hopes and expectations for the future. It was rarely claimed that poverty per se was to blame. Rather, the concern was with the culture of unemployment that can emerge within communities that have undergone economic decline, or within individual families in which there has been unemployment over several generations:

> It's third or fourth generation unemployment.... Their dads didn't work, their grandfathers didn't work, and that's a way of life. That's all they know. If you're brought up in a family that gets up in the morning, puts the TV on and has a beer and a fag, that's normal. It's not normal to get up and go to work. (Westerncity ASB coordinator)

This concern was expressed in a more extreme form by a Southcity housing officer, who talked of the neighbourhood as having been, 'an area of poverty for over 200 years; it is almost like it is in the water, it's in the blood of the people that they are deprived or something'. Unemployment and poverty over the generations were said by some to produce apathy and individualism:

> There's no sense of either personal or community responsibility.... There's no sense that the generation before did anything at all within the world to make it a better place for the young people of today, and therefore they have no need to do it for the next lot. (Southcity community association director)

'Kids will be kids'

The third set of explanations for ASB rests on the assumption that the misbehaviour is, in itself, not necessarily very problematic and is not necessarily getting worse. The main argument here is that while there undoubtedly *are* problems with ASB, these problems tend to be exaggerated and overestimated. In particular, older people are said to overreact to relatively 'normal' mischievousness among younger people – behaviour referred to, for example, as 'high jinks ... just teasing and antagonising' (Westerncity youth worker) or 'a bit of fun, a bit of malarkey' (Midcity regeneration worker). A Westerncity community safety coordinator observed:

> Older people tend to be intolerant; they see young people as sort of an intrinsic threat. The fact that they're not engaged in positive and regimented activities they see as a negative factor.

In essence, the narrative is premised on the ideas that:

- young people are simply pushing the boundaries of acceptable behaviour as they grow up;
- in some cases other people overreact to this;

- young people's boredom often lies at the heart of the problem; and
- curtailed freedom causes conflict.

This narrative was articulated by a number of the agency representatives we interviewed in the three case-study sites – but was frequently combined with the 'disengagement' narrative. In other words, many of the professionals appeared to believe that ASB can be explained partly in terms of the disengagement of young people; but that, at the same time, local people are more worried about ASB than they need to be. Some of the residents in interviews and focus groups also spoke about ASB in terms of 'kids will be kids' – while voicing their 'disengagement' and 'decline' concerns as well. Unsurprisingly, the 'purest' version of the 'kids will be kids' narrative was articulated in the focus groups with young people.

From the 'kids will be kids' perspective, fear and suspicion of young people's behaviour is often more of a problem than the behaviour itself. In two of the neighbourhoods we were told an identical story about how a respondent's acquaintance, when walking down the road, saw a gang of young people and crossed to the other side to avoid them. Having passed the group, she then noticed that her own son was among them, and realised that she had been needlessly intimidated. It is interesting that we heard the identical anecdote in two locations – which might suggest that it is an 'urban myth', freely used to illustrate the unfounded fears of older people.

Some respondents argued that overreaction to mild misbehaviour of children and young people is a result of the current climate of heightened anxiety about ASB. In other words, if concern about ASB has risen over the past few years, this is because the *social context* of the behaviour has changed rather than the behaviour itself. A Midcity community development worker argued that the 'paranoia' that exists today 'allows people to label anything they don't like as anti-social behaviour'. Taking this point further, it was argued that the labelling of youth activity as anti-social has a negative impact on the young people:

> Very often young people are vilified literally just for hanging out in large groups: people expect the worst. I am not saying that ASB doesn't go on in the area, but I certainly think that young people can become victims of the fear of crime. (Southcity community development worker)

The changing context of behaviour was also alluded to by a participant in the Midcity parents' focus group, who commented: 'Now you're not even allowed to play football on the street *because that's anti-social behaviour* and irritates the neighbours' (emphasis added). The argument here is that today, the act of playing football is something other than it seems: it is, in fact, ASB. When the participants in the Midcity young people's focus group were asked why they did not use the local playing fields, one responded:

> Playing fields! We're not even allowed to go on there and play football. Guarantee it, if you go on that field and play football you get arrested or something. It's just used for dogs shitting on – I'm being serious.

It was also suggested that the context of youth misbehaviour has changed not only in terms of heightened anxiety about ASB, but also in the sense that adults (as we have already seen) feel less able to intervene; and therefore the misbehaviour, in itself, is perceived as more threatening. A Midcity police sergeant argued:

> People don't know who lives next door to them, and they don't know whose kids are out on the street.... Kids hanging around on the street, that's a big problem, but kids have always done that. But why now is that a big problem? I think some of that is due to the fact that people don't know who those kids are. They've got no one to complain to.

As noted earlier, 'boredom/not enough to do' was said to be a cause of ASB by 58% of our ONS respondents. This explanation for ASB was frequently offered by respondents who articulated the 'kids will be kids' narrative:

> There's very little for them to do, so there's nothing to take them off the streets. So they're hanging around in the evenings, you know, bored. That's when they start making youth annoyance,

> criminal damage. (Westerncity Police Community Support Officer)

Many of our young focus group participants complained about boredom. For example, in Southcity: 'Like we're not on the streets out of choice you know, it's cold on the streets'. And in Westerncity: 'They [young people] just muck about in the field because that's the only space – they are always being told, "You can't go there, you can't go there"'.

Several respondents pointed out that young people have always sought to engage in risky or daring behaviour, and that part of growing up is about pushing the limits of what is acceptable. A youth worker in Westerncity noted: 'I don't think [young people] have got a clue what is anti-social and what is not.... Having a chase with the police is fun, that's the way they see it.' Several respondents emphasised also that peer pressure can play an important part in youth behaviour at the limits of acceptability.

A related point occasionally made was that today young people's freedoms are curtailed because of parental anxieties and, as a result, it is more difficult for them to express themselves and be rowdy without coming into conflict with adults. (This is another way in which the context of youth behaviour, rather than the behaviour itself, may have changed.) A Midcity police constable observed:

> On a number of occasions I have spoken with these lads who said, "Where else can you play?". Their parents don't let them play in areas such as [named] Country Park or where they're out of sight. If they're playing on the street they get complaints from other residents because of the nature of the place.

Several respondents emphasised that boredom propels young people towards misuse of drugs and alcohol – which can then contribute to local problems of ASB:

> Because they are bored, there is nothing to do. It's mainly drugs, crack and that. Other people burn cars and that, but crack is the biggest problem around here. (Midcity young people's focus group)

> [Cannabis] is so accessible, so it becomes easier to use it rather than trying to find active things to do. There is nothing to do, so the temptation is around. (Southcity drugs worker)

Explaining ASB: the three narratives

This chapter has described three sets of explanation for ASB, which we refer to as three 'narratives' because all are rooted in broader understandings of social and cultural change. The first two narratives, which are quite closely interrelated, assume that problems of ASB are getting worse, because of a generalised process of social and moral decline, or because of the increasing disengagement of a minority of British youth and/or their families. The third narrative, which asserts that most ASB is a matter of children and young people getting up to mischief, assumes that problems of ASB are not necessarily getting worse in themselves, but that the *context* of youthful misbehaviour is changing, and as a result people have become more likely to perceive this behaviour as anti-social and to be fearful of it.

In the next chapter, we consider how these different narratives imply different kinds of solutions to ASB.

5

Responding to ASB: the options

A wide variety of opinions was expressed by respondents in the case-study neighbourhoods about how ASB can and should be tackled. From our analysis of the qualitative material, we learnt that the suggested responses to ASB were – unsurprisingly – shaped by how respondents tended to explain the phenomenon. It should be noted that given the emphasis in the three neighbourhoods on manifestations of, and explanations for, youth ASB, the discussion of responses likewise tended to focus on children and young people.

This chapter considers the implications for policy of the three ASB narratives. Before presenting this material it is worth reiterating that the narratives very rarely, if ever, were articulated in a 'pure' form. Rather, most respondents expressed elements of different narratives simultaneously, while tending broadly to emphasise one more than the others. Hence, when we talk here about the policy implications of the narratives, we are not suggesting that most respondents spoke in terms of a single solution to a distinct set of problems. Our aim in this chapter is to highlight the connections between different kinds of explanation for, and different kinds of response to, ASB. In doing this, we are simplifying the complex and often ambiguous accounts provided by the respondents.

The narrative of decline: can enforcement help?

By definition, the narrative of decline is a highly pessimistic perspective on ASB. It implies that there are no ready solutions to the problems of ASB – unless any government were to acquire the ability to turn back the clock. Some focus group participants called for a radical approach to enforcement and punishment, as the only possible way of reversing the tide:

R1 Something has to be done because it's out of hand.
R2 But it's not going to get any better until there's a deterrent, because they can't smack them or anything. They should send them to a boot camp and give them a jolly good shaking, not just slap their hand and say, "Go and be a good boy or girl", or take them on holiday.
R1 That place in Middlesbrough sorted it out – why can't they try that here? ... Zero tolerance, that's what we want.
R3 But we're becoming a do-gooder society.
(Midcity retired people's focus group)

R1 Send them to Borstal, like they used do.
R2 They should go to prison, but they come out of there knowing how to burgle – it's like being at camp, I've heard. They get it too easy.
R3 It's not. I've been. It's not like being at camp.
(Midcity parents' focus group)

A strong theme that emerged in the parents' and retired people's focus groups was the participants' deep cynicism about current efforts by central government and local agencies to tackle ASB. While many appeared to be in favour of some form of enforcement, they often had little faith in the ability of national government or local agencies to bring about real change for the better. Many participants were aware that a number of new enforcement initiatives have been launched by government to tackle ASB, but were dismissive of these on the grounds that they were likely to be ineffective. The following quotations from focus groups illustrate this apparent disaffection with current policy – and also the respondents' awareness of government efforts to promote and publicise their new initiatives.

> What are these community police? To the best of my knowledge, they don't have any powers of arrest, they are walking around. And David Blunkett could say, "Put more police on the street", but you might as well put the boy scouts out there. Boy scouts would say, "Could you stop doing that please", and the second word would be "off" and there is nothing they can do about it. (Southcity parents' focus group)

> Mr Blunkett has been on television advertising [ASBOs], but on the ground, this is what we're talking about, they're supposed to happen on the ground and it's not, not at the moment. Listening to them it's happening straight away but I'm sorry sir, it's not, you can't change the culture overnight. (Westerncity retired people's focus group)

> If you have one of those anti-social behaviour orders on you, nationwide, how is that enforceable? ... It's another thing to stick in the newspapers to make it look like something is being done about it. (Southcity parents' focus group)

> You hear from the ministers that they are dealing with anti-social behaviour by using curfews, but where are the curfews? That's never been imposed – you never see them imposed; you hear about these things on television but you never see them on the ground. There is nothing being done – councils, police and the supposed security people don't come together. (Southcity retired people's focus group)

The despairing view of current policy was summed up by a Westerncity community activist: 'Up there in government they're giving the powers about public nuisance and all this, but there's nobody in authority using it. Nobody can do nothing; nobody knows nothing.'

In contrast to the general cynicism about new initiatives emanating from central government, there were a few signs of optimism about the capacity of communities to mobilise themselves against ASB. In Westerncity, some participants in the retired people's focus group argued that things had improved in the area because the tenants' association and others had made the decision to move things forward for themselves – in the absence of help from the authorities:

> In a lot of places things have been brought about because residents have got together to get these orders or get a family moved – it's not coming from authority, it's residents themselves who have banded together and said, "I'm not going to put up with this any longer", and they're the ones who have pushed it.

In Southcity, a community activist described a local movement, which – 'much to the chagrin of the police' – successfully drove out a local drug dealer. The dealer, he said, had been selling drugs when children were coming home from school:

> So the local residents got very cross with this 'cos the police would do nothing; and they all got placards – "drug dealers out" – and whistles, and I eventually joined this with my wife, and every time we saw him we waved the placards and blew the whistles and he ran off. I'm now told that he is dealing in another part of the area, not anywhere near us.

A somewhat different perspective on community action was evident in the Midcity parents' focus group. An argument voiced here was not so much that the community must take action when agencies fail; but, rather, that it is the responsibility of the community to sort out its own problems (by whatever means):

R1 A lot of people around here have been brought up to not phone the police and just deal with it yourself.

R2 It's like protecting your kids. If somebody's going to whack my kid then I'm sorry but I will whack *them*, because I am there to protect my kids.

In contrast, other focus group participants had little or no faith in any kind of self-policing capacity of the local community. In the retired people's focus group in Midcity, for example, there was general agreement that 'there's no community feeling now, not like it used to be' – thanks to the selfishness and 'I'm all right, Jack' attitudes of individuals in Britain today.

The disengagement narrative: promoting engagement

For those who explain problems of ASB largely in terms of the 'disengagement' of the perpetrators, the logical implication is that these problems will be reduced if agencies can manage to reintegrate the most marginalised individuals and families within their local communities and wider society. Respondents who spoke in these terms tended to focus – singly or in combination – on early intervention (including support for parenting), intensive youth work and community partnership as the main ways in which this process of reintegration can be carried out. They frequently stressed the need for long-term funding and support for these kinds of initiatives, and complained that the short-termism of much current funding limits the capacity of programmes to achieve their aims of addressing the underlying problems that cause ASB. Effective enforcement was said to be a necessary element of work aiming at reintegration, although respondents also spoke of the risks associated with enforcement.

Several respondents talked about early intervention as an essential – or even *the* essential – element of work targeting the familial problems that produce ASB. 'If we are going to make a long-term difference with young people, it doesn't start when they are 12; it's got to start when they are two or three or four', commented a Midcity community development worker. The local MP also talked of the need to 'rigorously target' those aged up to five, in order 'to give them their life chance'. He also said that it is vital to work with parents before their children are even born.

Again in Midcity, a Sure Start worker talked about the critical importance of working with parents who 'live very difficult lives and find parenting quite difficult at times'. This kind of work can have a significant impact on the parents' confidence, and consequently on the behaviour of their children. Two family project workers in Westerncity spoke about their experience of seeing very tangible changes in the families and children they have worked with. The parents, they have found, have become more confident in dealing with their children; and teachers at local schools have reported that they have seen changes in the children's ability to cope. The project's approach is based on the assumption that many of the parents have themselves been poorly parented and therefore need help; but, at the same time, these parents must be able to take responsibility for their own children.

As we have seen, many respondents in the case-study neighbourhoods strongly argued that the root causes of much ASB is the incapacity of young people to engage constructively and meaningfully with those around them. To address this problem – these respondents frequently stressed – is difficult, and takes time, energy and commitment.

Constructive work with youth is believed to involve changing attitudes and building capacity. This partly entails finding what activities the young people are genuinely interested in, and encouraging them to work on these activities. According to a project coordinator in Westerncity, much of this work has the overarching aim of building connections with young people who have previously made few connections with anyone:

> The approach towards these young people is mutual respect. And half the problem is these youngsters have never been treated that way. They wouldn't have been treated that way in school, their neighbours see them as a pain in the backside and tell them that's what they are, to that effect, and they retaliate accordingly then. So it's trying to break that cycle.

A Southcity Youth Inclusion Project (YIP) manager also talked about seeing positive changes in young people with serious behavioural problems – but emphasised that these changes take time to occur, and usually are the result of intensive, one-to-one work. The workers need to spend a lot of time with the young people – building boundaries, establishing respect, and also helping them to find their niche and their own particular interests. Residential trips with the young people on the YIP, he said, can provide a particularly good opportunity for workers to make real inroads.

Community involvement was cited by several respondents as an important element of work to reintegrate the more excluded young people and families. From this perspective, community involvement is seen in terms of partnership between the local community and the statutory agencies (and not so much, as in the example discussed above of the drug dealer driven out of Southcity, as a matter of residents taking affairs into their own hands, in the belief that the statutory agencies are achieving nothing). Among other things, this kind of partnership can involve engaging young people by working with them *from within the community* and not just through external agencies.

For example, we were told about a project in Westerncity which took the form of a 'community house' established by a local resident, with the support of the council. This project targeted local teenagers who were getting into trouble, and apparently had some success in building relationships with them. The project also undertook wider community development work, but retained its voluntary status and local focus. The head of the Westerncity housing department, talking about community work more generally, commented that local residents had been cynical about what the statutory agencies were doing; but that a sense of partnership between the agencies and the community had eventually emerged:

> It did take an awful lot of meetings with them, talking through the issues, and demonstrating to them that we have the commitment to turn the estates round with them. And that can only happen through building up the trust and working with the communities.

In the other two neighbourhoods also, respondents from key agencies spoke about the critical importance of community involvement in ASB work. In all three areas, it was widely recognised that effective community partnership depends a great deal on the energy, commitment – and often charisma – of individual residents. The success of the 'community house' in Westerncity, for example, was largely attributed to the hard work of the woman who had launched it. In Southcity we spoke with a community activist who evidently was prepared to devote considerable amounts of time to mobilising other residents and working with the police and other agencies. Like those involved in the Westerncity community house, she also put effort into establishing links with children and young people, and involving the young people themselves in community work. However, she stressed that the fear of retaliation was something that she had to live with:

> I've been threatened – "I'm gonna cut your throat" ... they've thrown stuff at my windows ... loads of verbal abuse. I've been called a grass – every swearword you wanna come up with. But that's all right – all I say to them is get a life. But that doesn't mean I'm not frightened. And my daughter's frightened for me....

Agency representatives who articulated the disengagement narrative often saw an important role for enforcement – as a necessary part of the work of engaging youth. It was argued that enforcement helps to provide 'boundaries' or 'structure' in the lives of young people who previously have been left to do whatever they wanted. Respondents also noted that enforcement action, when it is needed, should be implemented quickly and effectively: empty threats, and unenforced ASBOs, can be counterproductive:

> In extreme circumstances there needs to be [a threat] ... when the softly, softly approach doesn't have any effect. But it also needs to be seen to be *done* as well. I think threat isn't always sufficient. If it's going to happen it needs to be put into action; that it's not an idle threat. (Westerncity project coordinator)

It was also suggested that enforcement can be a way of getting through to parents who otherwise take little interest in their children:

> When you fine parents, it occurs to them that they could lose their house – it focuses their mind remarkably well. They certainly develop more of an interest in their young people and what they are doing. (Westerncity community safety coordinator)

However, respondents also raised concerns about the effects of enforcement, and indicated that there is deep-seated ambivalence among practitioners about current practice. It was suggested that some enforcement measures will be counterproductive, if they have the effect of further alienating those who are already alienated:

> If you have the label of having had one ASBO, does that follow you forever? I think people should have to take responsibility for their actions and they should realise that their behaviour has an impact. But to put their picture in the papers – you probably have to be really, really awful; but you see those tense little faces and you just think … "You are hell but you must have been through hell". (Midcity family worker)

The Westerncity ASB coordinator talked about the importance of a graduated approach to enforcement, when discussing a local ASB perpetrator who was only 10-years-old:

> We thought that if we put an ASBO on him, yes he will probably end up in the criminal justice system in a few years time – but if we ASBO him now he's going to end up there an awful lot quicker because he will breach it. So we're going to work with him for a little bit longer and see what happens. If there's no other way, we will have to use it, but it's our final straw.

Some respondents pointed out that certain forms of enforcement – for example, use of dispersal orders – are likely to displace rather than reduce incidents of ASB. More generally, a number of respondents argued that the main problem with enforcement is that it deals with the symptoms rather than the causes of ASB, and hence cannot resolve local problems:

> It's about dog patrols; it's about PCSOs [Police Community Support Officers]; about high visibility stuff. It's not a lot about what I would call the softer side of things – actually dealing with the root causes…. It's about getting the little blighters on the street and telling them what's what, and scaring them. And that isn't really what we should be about. (Southcity community safety officer)

> If anything is a sign of government failure, it is the sign of having to keep putting more police on the street. Yet that is seen now as something positive. (Midcity partnership worker)

The 'kids will be kids' narrative: the need for diversion

The 'kids will be kids' narrative is partly based on the assumption that concerns about ASB arise out of mistrust and misunderstanding between the generations. Therefore one implication of this narrative is that in order to reduce concerns about ASB, there needs to be greater intergenerational dialogue and negotiation. A small number of respondents made this point explicitly, for example:

> Part of the problem will be modifying the expectations of the complainant: people who are unreasonably intolerant. (Westerncity community safety coordinator)

> I think we need to do more generational work. I think kids hanging out on a street corner isn't necessarily intimidating or anti-social to me. But I have information because I have worked in that environment … and I can understand how people who don't have the information get intimidated. (Southcity community safety officer)

However, from the 'kids will be kids' perspective, respondents were much more likely to talk about the need for diversionary activities for young people than about the importance of building bridges between the generations. The assumption here was that if boredom and young people's natural tendency towards mischief are the major causes of perceived ASB, then the main answer to the problem lies in the provision of exciting or challenging things for them to do. It was also frequently pointed out that the provision of *affordable* activities is crucial.

A few respondents referred to local diversionary schemes that had apparently been successful in addressing ASB: for example, a Midcity local councillor talked about a newly established boxing club that had 'defused the street problem'. More frequently, however, respondents talked about the current lack of provision – or pointed out that while some age groups were well-catered for, others had little to do. For example, the young focus group participants in both Midcity and Southcity talked about the need for youth clubs for people in their late teens. One respondent in the Midcity group also argued: 'What they need to do, is get about 50 bangers and put them all out on some country park, and that will keep everyone out of trouble that will, guaranteed'.

Participants in the Midcity parents' focus group had a similar view:

R1 Find something for the kids to do, give them one of those banger projects – get some old stock cars and make them make their own cars, give them the parts to fix the cars.
R2 They need to occupy their minds.
R3 Give the girls some singing lessons.
R2 Teach them dance, something for them all to do.
R4 Teach them some manners for one.

However, most of the respondents who spoke of the need for diversion also made it clear that this cannot provide the whole solution to the complex problem of ASB. Many talked of the difficulty of ensuring that the most troubled, and troublesome, youngsters get involved in whatever is made available. The Midcity ASB coordinator commented on the generally good youth provision in the area, but said that a lot of young people simply are not interested:

> Engaging in organised youth provision doesn't make money, whereas going out and robbing sheds makes money. Often it is more exciting to nick a car – it gets you more status with your peer group than going on a climbing expedition with whichever organisation.

It can be difficult to identify and provide activities that will genuinely appeal to certain young people: a warden from Midcity said that the greatest need in the area is for better facilities for the young; but when you ask them what they want, 'They say somewhere to race cars around, and somewhere to smoke cannabis'. Another difficulty is ensuring that young people behave responsibly when they attend local activities. A police constable in Midcity commented: 'If there was somewhere they could go where the parents would know they were safe, I am sure the majority of the kids would be absolutely fine; but it's the minority that will wreck the place and burn it down or steal from it'. A regeneration worker in Midcity talked of the work they had put into the local park:

> We fought really hard to get a good facility in the area. We got it "green flag" status, which means that it was upgraded.... Little buggers have wrecked it. But we won't be perturbed, we keep on putting new equipment in and we've got "green flag" for a second year.

A potentially more deep-seated problem with diversion was raised by a community development worker in Midcity. He argued that the provision of too many activities can, in itself, be problematic and even counterproductive, because 'you create this dependency culture where every evening will be filled with all these wonderful activities'. This then produces a belief that 'you need to occupy these young people because if you don't occupy them they are obviously going to get into trouble. And I think we have got a serious problem in society if we accept that it's true.'

From the 'kids will be kids' perspective – as from the 'disengagement' perspective – enforcement measures against ASB carry some risks; although few denied that enforcement is needed to halt the worst excesses of youthful misbehaviour.

For those who believe that much of what is assumed to be ASB is not in fact seriously harmful, many of the enforcement remedies currently deployed are too punitive, and amount to an overreaction to the perceived problems. For example, a partnership worker in Midcity said of dispersal orders:

> Four lads can stand on a street corner talking and a police van can roll up and say: "You look a bit suspicious to me – get in this van – we're taking you home because it is half past nine". How can that be right in a democracy? How can you do that? It's outrageous, absolutely outrageous.

A participant in the Midcity parents' focus group had similar concerns: 'Even if the kids aren't doing anything the police still bother them. I have two 14-year-olds and the police are always coming up to them because they're hanging around.'

This viewpoint was most strongly expressed by some of the young people in the focus groups – as might be expected. However, the young people's objections to enforcement perhaps cannot be dismissed as predictably defensive responses. Given that definitions of ASB are unclear, and that the harms caused by ASB are often more to do with exaggerated (if understandable) fear than with reality, there are bound to be questions asked about the appropriateness of prohibiting certain forms of perceived ASB. Examples of young people's comments about being unfairly targeted by enforcement activity include the following, from Midcity and Southcity respectively:

> There were local criminals standing around – I walked up the street with them and got an anti-social behaviour order for that … and if you ask me that's a load of shit, walking up the street with somebody.

> [The police] are trying [to crack down on ASB] because they've got all their little community support officers out there.... But I think they just need to sort out the big-time people before they come with little petty things. You know, with people being in gangs – not even in gangs, but just a group of people. They'll come and start on them instead of walking another few minutes up the road to get someone who's got a knife or whatever.

ASB responses: concluding remarks

Our interviews and focus groups in the case-study neighbourhoods brought to light an extremely wide range of opinions on what can and should be done about ASB. Unsurprisingly, we found that respondents' views on ASB responses were largely informed by how they understood the phenomenon: in other words, each of the three 'narratives' of ASB have different implications for practice.

Those who hold to a narrative of decline tend to be more strongly in favour of enforcement in theory than those with other views, but they also tend to be cynical about the efficacy of current efforts to reduce ASB in practice. They also see little hope in alternative approaches other than, possibly, community mobilisation against ASB perpetrators. For those who largely view ASB in terms of the 'disengagement' of certain young people and their families, work that takes the form of early intervention, intensive youth work, parenting support and community partnership offers some promise. From this perspective, enforcement is a necessary element of local ASB initiatives, but must be used selectively and with great care. The 'kids will be kids' narrative implies that the provision of genuinely attractive and affordable diversionary activities for young people should be the cornerstone of local ASB strategies – although targeted and proportionate enforcement should also play a part.

6

Conclusions: implications for policy and practice

This study has assembled a great deal of information about the ways that people experience ASB and talk about its causes and potential solutions. In this concluding chapter we draw out the lessons for policy and practice. These lessons concern:

- the analysis pf problems of ASB;
- the search for solutions;
- the management of local action on ASB;
- the handling of public opinion.

Analysing problems of ASB

We have seen that people use three separate 'narratives' to talk about ASB – although all of these tend largely to equate ASB with misbehaviour by young people. First, and probably the dominant narrative among the general public, is the decline of standards of behaviour. The second narrative, and the one professionals tended to emphasise, centres on the processes of social exclusion that lead to groups of disengaged young people. Third, and perhaps reflecting a more tolerant stance, is the view that young people always have, and always will, behave badly as they challenge societal norms during their transition to adulthood.

We have *not* suggested that people divide into three groups, according to the explanations for ASB that they favour. Certainly there were some people who relied on a single narrative to make sense of their experience of ASB – but many often switched between narratives. However, a different set of assumptions is embedded in each, and a different set of conclusions flows from each. As we discussed in Chapter 5, explanations for ASB that emphasise social exclusion will obviously point to inclusionary solutions.

Perhaps a little less obviously, the language of declining standards orientates people to solutions that involve tougher discipline and greater emphasis on individual responsibility. And the more that ASB is a reminder of the cultural universal that 'kids will be kids', the more the solutions will lie in patience, tolerance and diversionary strategies for steering people through their adolescence with minimum disruption to all.

This analysis poses the obvious question, 'Which narrative is right?' Some differences between the three narratives are, in principle at least, open to empirical test. The narratives of declining standards and of social exclusion share the assumption that ASB is on the increase. By contrast the suggestion that 'kids will be kids' implies that our increasing concern about ASB reflects not objective changes, but changes in our capacity to tolerate disorder and incivility.

We do not propose to discuss in detail how one might adjudicate between these two claims. Nonetheless, two things are worth pointing out. The balance of probability is that at the start of the 21st century our tolerance for violence is now very much lower than it was 50 or 100 years ago. Pub brawls and domestic violence are no longer culturally embedded into the lives of many social groups. On the other hand, only the most myopic of social historians could ignore the decline over several decades of youthful deference, coupled with the emergence of forms of consumerist hedonism, especially those concerned with alcohol and drug use. We may not live in more violent times than our parents or grandparents, but for better or worse, we probably do lead less regulated and less orderly lives, in an age of increasing mobility and family breakdown.

It is much harder to say whether a growth in ASB – or at least a decline in orderliness – is better understood in terms of a general decline in standards, or in terms of the social exclusion of some groups that is created by the growing inequalities of 21st-century life. The most important set of findings to emerge from Chapter 2 is that the vast majority of the population do *not* suffer significantly from ASB. Rather, a minority have their lives affected by ASB, and a very small minority find that their lives are truly blighted by it. Arguably, this lends weight to the narrative of social exclusion – where the losers in a 'winner takes all' society create truly troublesome problems for others. On the other hand, one might explain the concentration of ASB among the socially deprived simply as the tip of the iceberg of social and moral decline.

We conclude that factual evidence will shed only limited light on the debate about the causes of ASB. After all, criminal policy and criminology have been grappling with similar questions for decades, trying to strike a constructive balance between the language of blame and the language of criminal causation in dealing with people who are certainly moral agents, but whose self-command is often limited, and sometimes very limited indeed. Perhaps the important point to recognise is that the emergence of ASB as a policy concern has led to a re-emergence of the debate about criminal (or legal) responsibility in a reshaped and slightly reformulated way. The population of ASB perpetrators certainly overlaps very extensively with the population that provides the criminal courts with their staple diet. What political and media debate about ASB has done is to reinvigorate the narrative about declining standards – with its implicit call for tougher discipline – by finding a new set of graphic illustrations of malice causing pain to the innocent.

This analysis is not intended to make light of the distress caused to those who are the victims of ASB. On the contrary, we suggest that loosely deployed rhetoric about 'mindless louts' and 'neighbours from hell' can stand in the way of understanding the origins and nature of such problems and thus can block effective solutions. It is important to understand the processes that lead neighbourhoods to lose their social capital – or their capacity to sustain standards of civility and cooperation.[19] That sense of powerlessness besetting our least advantaged communities is a reflection partly of cultural shifts, and partly of the unintended consequences of several decades of social, economic and policing policy. In finding solutions to ASB problems, this range of factors must not be ignored.

The search for solutions

This study has involved *analysis* of approaches to tackling ASB, but we cannot claim to have *evaluated* what works and what does not. Our original intention was to 'compare and contrast' ASB strategies that struck very different balances between enforcement and prevention. We had hoped that some systematic differences might emerge between areas that could be tied to strategies for tackling ASB. However, our starting premise was not supported. The similarities between the responses to ASB in the three areas were greater than the differences. The area that was selected for its privileging of enforcement turned out to have a 'mixed economy' in which there was significant investment in prevention. The area selected for its emphasis on prevention had well-developed systems for enforcement. And the area representing the middle ground did indeed show a balance – but no more than our supposed outliers. Even if we had found significant natural variation, however, we would have been hard-pressed to say whether one area had found the best balance. What we can do, however, is reflect the experiences of those who were responsible for tackling ASB in these neighbourhoods on a daily basis. Several interrelated points are worth emphasising.

First, we were struck by the sharp contrast between the push to prioritise enforcement at a national level, and concerns about the risks of enforcement and commitment to preventive options, at local levels. This is not totally surprising: the national TOGETHER initiative is, after all, a time-limited *campaign*, intended to respond to public concerns, to reduce public preparedness to tolerate ASB, to increase public expectations about the level of response from local authorities and police, and to spur these

[19] It is contestable whether the 'bonding capital' of neighbourhoods is depleted by exposure to disadvantage, but it is easy to see how their 'bridging capital' could be eroded (cf Putnam, 2000)

agencies into action. To communicate these messages clearly, TOGETHER uses simple, populist language, justifying tough enforcement, for example, as 'being on the side of the victim'. As the campaign begins to draw to a close, it is to be hoped that in its policy analysis, at least, the Home Office will feel able to adopt a more balanced position. Even critics of rigorous enforcement can be 'on the side of the victim'. While the TOGETHER campaign can be applauded for asserting the critical importance of supporting ASB victims, it is fair to question the assumption that support for victims necessarily implies a favouring of enforcement over preventive measures.

Second, we got a very clear sense from local professionals of the relative intractability of problems of disorder in areas facing extensive social deprivation. They did not conceptualise ASB simply as a problem of predation on the 'law-abiding majority' on the part of perpetrators, but as forms of conflict within communities with limited social capital or low collective efficacy. Not surprisingly, they tended to see enforcement as only one element within the set of remedies needed to rebuild these communities. They also stressed the need for long-term investment in rebuilding communities.

Third, as we discussed in Chapter 4, the professionals we interviewed tended to use the 'disengagement' narrative in describing the challenges and difficulties of engaging young people. Those most involved in ASB were described as young people with limited personal resources, living in areas offering limited opportunities. Enforcement tactics may contain their misbehaviour in the short term, but for the longer term, enforcement clearly needs to be balanced with inclusionary measures.

Fourth, in areas most beset by ASB, ways have to be found of countering the sense of powerlessness, and accompanying entrenched pessimism, among residents (especially older residents). There is a need to break the vicious circle whereby fears and expectations of ASB, fear of retaliation, lack of faith in the authorities' capacity to do anything, and incidents of ASB (and so on) all reinforce each other. Visible enforcement action may provide the leverage to do so, although it seems likely that community capacity-building measures will also be needed.

Finally, it will be remembered that both residents and professionals frequently deployed the 'kids will be kids' narrative in explaining ASB. It is obviously important to avoid a sort of 'net widening' whereby formal action is taken against relatively minor forms of misbehaviour that have been tolerated for generations.

Whether or not they use the terminology, we have seen clear agreement among professionals that long-term solutions to ASB necessarily involve the rebuilding of social capital in those – socially and economically deprived – areas that are most susceptible to ASB problems. Two themes emerged here. The first is that success or failure in mobilising communities will depend very much on the personal qualities and authority of staff involved. We were repeatedly told that just one good worker can make all the difference, and that neighbourhood 'champions' were essential, whether they were local residents or professionals from agencies. People with these qualities are, of course, a scarce resource.

The second – and related – theme is that outsiders can only go so far in developing and supporting systems of informal social control. Communities may feel powerless, but *imposing*, or 'parachuting', solutions is no solution at all. It is hard to avoid the conclusion that developing or recovering social capital in such communities is a slow, delicate process, involving sustained commitment and long-term investment – both from agencies and from neighbourhoods.

Managing local action on ASB

Chapter 5 and Appendix B of this report describe the very wide range of ASB activity in our three sites. In all three, a great deal of energy and investment had been deployed, but it was hard to discern extensive coordination between agencies or between departments within agencies. Indeed, in Appendix B we found it easy to list *activities* in hand to tackle ASB, but hard to summarise the overarching strategy in each area. Although we cannot prove that better coordination would pay off, we were left with a very clear sense that there was a need for:

- shared definitions of ASB to inform approaches to and the parameters around the issues to be tackled at a local level;

- a shared understanding of the underlying factors to inform responses;
- better coordination between projects in developing strategies and taking action; and
- better integration of ASB work within neighbourhood renewal strategies.

As local ASB coordinators become more settled in their posts (provided their positions are properly resourced and supported within their Crime and Disorder Reduction Partnerships), and the development of local ASB strategies is advanced, it may be possible for these needs to be met.

If residents have been let down in the past, or do not trust projects to deliver – no matter how coordinated or integrated activity is – the potential for success is limited. Purdue (2001, p 2222) has observed that, 'all too often they [community leaders] were expected to trust their powerful partners without reciprocation'. In the case-study areas, projects or ASB strategies were sometimes 'parachuted in' with minimal regard for the views or experiences of residents. Hughes (2004, p 17) has put it thus:

> The people who live in high crime areas have been incidental rather than central to "community" crime prevention efforts. As a consequence, agencies charged with constructing community-based programmes have largely ignored the core constituency and then determine that it cannot be relied on as an agent of change.

We think there is certainly scope for the development of a shared governance of ASB strategies in these areas – shared between neighbourhood residents *and* the agencies working for them – while acknowledging the difficulties in identifying truly representative community leaders (see Sampson et al, 1988; Jones and Newburn, 2001). But the benefits could outweigh such difficulties in improving collective efficacy. It is a question of who governs ASB in neighbourhoods.

We would stress the importance of putting more effort into developing shared definitions of ASB. We appreciate that the TOGETHER campaign has tended to avoid doing so, not wishing to curb artificially the range of uses to which the new measures for tackling ASB could be used. Now that the need for action against ASB is more widely accepted, it is time for agencies to be clearer about the ambit of the term ASB. The first reason for doing so is simple: if local authorities and the police put in place strategies for dealing with ASB, they need to commit resources to these strategies, clarify responsibilities across agencies and manage the performance of those delivering the strategy. This cannot be done unless there is more clarity about where ASB begins and where it ends.

The second reason for attending more closely to definitions is more subtle. The new ASB remedies include some sweeping powers. Civil law measures such as ASBOs supplement the criminal law system of deterrent threat with personalised deterrent threats tailor-made to specific perpetrators. If the threats are ignored, the penalty (potentially up to five years' imprisonment) can be heavy. In our view, the universality of the criminal law is an important principle of justice: we are all exposed to the same array of deterrent threats that are embedded in the criminal law. The principle of universality should be abandoned only under clearly specified circumstances. We think it important to develop much more explicit rationales for justifying the deployment of powerful civil law remedies – in order to set agreed limits to their use.

Handling public opinion

Our final set of conclusions relates to public opinion about ASB. The government's TOGETHER strategy appeals centrally to the narrative of declining standards that we identified in Chapter 3. The strategy launch in late 2003 used video footage to illustrate graphically how people's lives can be ruined by ASB – and how some people can find the resilience and real moral courage to fight back against the threat posed by this sort of behaviour. After the video had been screened, the audience was asked to give a standing ovation for the survivors of ASB in the video.

Those who 'take a stand' in this way against declining standards in their neighbourhoods fully deserve our respect. Few, if any, of the readers of this report will find themselves facing such nightmares. Whether government policy should be marketed in this way, however, is questionable. The launch was designed to overwhelm any questions about the need for this particular form of ASB strategy. It painted a stark conflict between innocent victims and mindless thuggery. In keynote speeches, fairly explicit warnings were given that professionals in local agencies would be held to account if they proved reluctant to use the new ASB armoury. There were no shades of grey in the way that the problem was portrayed and little subtlety in the range of solutions offered.

Earlier in this chapter we suggested that effective ASB strategies need to recognise the factors that underlie ASB. As we suggested at the start of this report, these factors are likely to involve a complex interaction between social policies, economic policies and policing priorities. The unintended consequences of these policies, in terms of ASB, have borne down hard on Britain's most disadvantaged communities. To conclude the chapter, we want to examine the potential costs of what we see as an oversimplified political and media debate about ASB.

The TOGETHER campaign draws on the 'declining standards' narrative to offer images of the struggle between ordinary decent folk and the tide of loutishness. As a means of mobilising agencies to action it has much to recommend itself. One can sympathise with a government that is impatient for action but unable to get its hands directly on the levers for action. As a means of mobilising agencies to action, the TOGETHER campaign has much to recommend itself. The public presentation of the campaign:

- resonates with real public anxieties about declining standards;
- cogently reshapes these worries into a sense of vulnerability in the face of pressing threats to social order; and
- presents the image of tough, resolute government action responding to these threats.

Whether it is good politics to adopt and legitimate the narrative of 'falling standards' is another matter. Fuelling public concerns about social order in this way pays off – in terms of electoral gain – only if the tough, resolute response is fully persuasive. In Chapter 5 we discussed how the 'declining standards' narrative was infused with a deep sense of pessimism about the scope for solutions of any sort, and in particular a well-entrenched cynicism about the likelihood of an effective local authority response. Our judgment is that the media and presentational elements of the TOGETHER campaign will succeed in fuelling public anxieties and playing on existing fears, but will fail to present a persuasive government response.

It will be remembered from Chapter 4 that people did not subscribe simply to one or other narrative about ASB. Not only professionals but the residents we interviewed often recognised the complexity of the factors underlying ASB. The government might do better to present its ASB strategies in ways that recognise the need to be not only tough on ASB but tough on the causes of ASB.

References

Blair, T. (2003) PM speech on anti-social behaviour, QEII Centre, London, 14 October (www.pm.gov.uk/output/Page4644.asp).

Blunkett, D. (2003) 'Civil renewal: a new agenda', The CSV Edith Kahn Memorial Lecture, 11 June (www.homeoffice.gov.uk/docs2/civilrennewagenda.pdf).

Clancy, A., Hough, M., Aust, R. and Kershaw, K. (2001) *Crime, policing and justice: Findings from the 2000 British Crime Survey*, Home Office Research Study 223, London: Home Office.

Cohen, L.E. and Felson, M. (1979) 'Social change and crime rate trends: a routine activity approach', *American Sociological Review*, vol 44, pp 588-608.

Fairnington, A. (2004) 'Communities that care: a case study of regeneration', *Critical Public Health*, vol 14, no 1, pp 27-36.

Felson, M. (1998) *Crime and everyday life* (2nd edn), Thousand Oaks, CA: Pine Forge Press.

Finney, A. and Toofail, J. (2004) 'Levels and trends', in T. Dodd, S. Nicholas, D. Povey and A. Walker (eds) *Crime in England and Wales 2003/2004*, London: Home Office.

FitzGerald, M., Hough, M., Joseph, I. and Qureshi, T. (2002) *Policing for London*, Cullompton, Devon: Willan Publishing.

France, A. and Crow, I. (2001) *CTC – The story so far: An interim evaluation of Communities that Care*, York: Joseph Rowntree Foundation/York Publishing Services.

GLA (Greater London Authority) (2004) *The London anti-social behaviour strategy: Proposals for consultation with stakeholders*, London: GLA.

Harradine, S., Kodz, J., Lernetti, F. and Jones, B. (2004) *Defining and measuring anti-social behaviour*, Home Office Development and Practice Report 26, London. Home Office.

Home Office (2001) *Policing a new century: A blueprint for reform*, Cm 5326, London: The Stationery Office.

Home Office (2002) *The national policing plan 2003-2006*, London: Home Office.

Home Office (2004a) *Building communities, beating crime: A better police service for the 21st century*, London: Home Office.

Home Office (2004b) *Confident communities in a secure Britain: The Home Office strategic plan 2004-08*, London: Home Office.

Hough, M. (2003) 'Modernisation and public opinion: some criminal justice paradoxes', *Contemporary Politics*, no 9, pp 143-55.

Hough, M. (2004) 'Modernisation, scientific rationalism and the crime reduction programme', *Criminal Justice*, vol 4, no 3, pp 239-53.

Hough, M. and Jacobson, J. (2004) 'Togetherness is a shared strategy? Getting to grips with anti-social behaviour', in J. Grieve and R. Howard (eds) *Communities, social exclusion and crime*, London: Smith Institute.

Hughes, G. (2004) 'The community governance of crime, justice and safety: challenges and lesson-drawing', *British Journal of Community Justice*, vol 2, no 3, pp 7-20.

Innes, M. (2004) 'Reinventing tradition? Reassurance, neighbourhood security and policing', *Criminal Justice*, vol 4, no 2, pp 151-71.

Innes, M. and Fielding, N. (2002) 'From community to communicative policing: 'signal crimes' and the problem of public reassurance', *Sociological Research Online*, vol 7, no 2 (www.socresonline.org.uk).

Jacobs, J. (1961) *The death and life of great American cities*, New York, NY: Random House.

Jacobson, J., Millie, A. and Hough, M. (forthcoming) *Tackling anti-social behaviour: A critical review*, London: ICPR, King's College London.

Jones, T. and Newburn, T. (2001) *Widening access: Improving public relations with hard to reach groups*, Police Research Series Paper 138, London: Home Office.

Kelling, G.L. and Coles, C.M. (1996) *Fixing broken windows: Restoring order and reducing crime in our communities*, New York, NY: Free Press.

Millie, A. and Herrington, V. (2005) 'Bridging the gap: understanding reassurance policing', *The Howard Journal of Criminal Justice*, vol 44, no 1, pp 41-56.

Millie, A., Jacobson, J., Hough, M. and Paraskevopoulou, A. (forthcoming) *Anti-social behaviour in London: Setting the context for the London anti-social behaviour strategy*, London: GLA.

Moore, L. and Yeo, H. (2004) *Crime in England and Wales 2003/4: London region*, Home Office Regional factsheet, London: Home Office.

Newman, O. (1972) *Defensible space: People and design in the violent city*, London: Architectural Press.

ODPM (Office of the Deputy Prime Minister) (2004) *Neighbourhood Management Pathfinder programme national evaluation: Annual review 2002/2003 Research Report*, Wetherby: ODPM.

Ove Arup (2000) *[Southcity] Neighbourhood Regeneration Strategy*, London: Ove Arup.

Phillips, T. and Smith, P. (2003) 'Everyday incivility: towards a benchmark', *The Sociological Review*, vol 51, no 1, pp 85-108.

Purdue, D. (2001) 'Neighbourhood governance: leadership, trust and social capital', *Urban Studies*, vol 38, no 12, pp 2211-24.

Putnam, R.D. (1994) 'What makes democracy work?', *Institute of Public Affairs Review*, vol 47, no 1, pp 31-4.

Putnam, R.D. (2000) *Bowling alone: The collapse and revival of American community*, New York, NY: Simon and Schuster.

Sampson, R.J. and Raudenbush, S.W. (1999) 'Systematic social observation of public spaces: a new look at disorder in urban neighbourhoods', *American Journal of Sociology*, no 105, pp 603-51.

Sampson, R.J., Raudenbush, S.W. and Earls, F. (1997) 'Neighbourhoods and violent crime: a multilevel study of collective efficacy', *Science*, no 277, pp 918-24.

Sampson, A., Stubbs, P., Smith, D., Pearson, G. and Blagg, H. (1988) 'Crime, localities and the multi-agency approach', *British Journal of Criminology*, no 28, pp 478-93.

Skogan, W. (1986) 'Fear of crime and neighbourhood change', in A.J. Reiss and M. Tonry (eds) *Communities and crime*, Chicago, IL: University of Chicago Press.

Skogan, W. (1990) *Disorder and decline: Crime and the spiral of decay in American neighbourhoods*, New York, NY: Free Press.

Skogan, W. and Hartnett, S. (1997) *Community policing, Chicago style*, New York, NY: Oxford University Press.

Skogan, W., Steiner, L., Dubois, J., Gudell, J.E. and Fagan, A. (2002) *Taking stock: Community policing in Chicago*, Washington, DC: National Institute of Justice.

Skogan, W., Steiner, L., Benitez, C., Dennis, J., Borchers, S., Dubois, J., Gondocs, R., Hartnett, S., Kim, S.Y. and Rosenbaum, S. (2004) *CAPS at ten: Community policing in Chicago: An evaluation of Chicago's alternative policing strategy*, Chicago, IL: Illinois Criminal Justice Information Authority.

Thorpe, K. and Wood, M. (2004) 'Antisocial behaviour', in S. Nicholas and A. Walker (eds) *Crime in England and Wales 2002/2003: Supplementary volume 2: Crime, disorder and the criminal justice system – Public attitudes and perceptions*, Home Office Statistical Bulletin 02/04, London: Home Office.

Wilson, J. and Kelling, G. (1982) 'Broken windows – the police and neighborhood safety', *The Atlantic Monthly*, March, no 249, pp 29-38.

Wood, M. (2004) Perceptions and experience of antisocial behaviour: Findings from the 2003/2004 British Crime Survey, Home Office Online Report 49/04, London: Home Office.

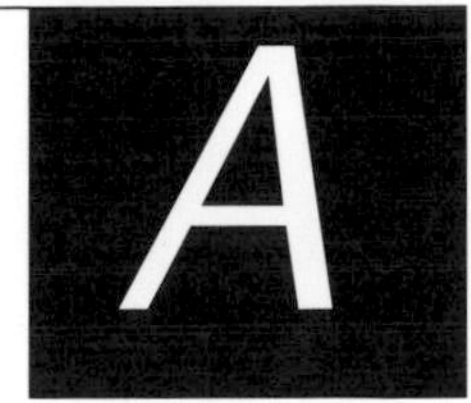

Appendix A: Survey questionnaire

Module 352 – Tackling Anti-Social Behaviour – King's College London

M352_Intro

The next set of questions is being asked on behalf of researchers at King's College London.

Ask if: QSETUP.ADTYPE = EVEN

M352_1a

In 2003, the government launched its strategy for tackling anti-social behaviour.

What do you think the government means by anti-social behaviour?

INTERVIEWER: Please record verbatim

Ask if: QSETUP.ADTYPE = ODD

M352_1b

SHOWCARD C352_1b

In 2003, the government launched its strategy for tackling anti-social behaviour.
Which of the areas on this card do you think the strategy is aiming to reduce?

INTERVIEWER: The following are definitely part of the strategy: noisy neighbours, graffiti, rowdy teenagers on the streets and possibly drug dealing.

Code all that apply

SET OF

(1)	NNbour	Noisy neighbours
(2)	DrugDeal	Drug dealing
(3)	Graff	Graffiti
(4)	Traffic	Traffic noise and pollution
(5)	Mugging	Mugging
(6)	Speed	Speeding
(7)	Teens	Rowdy teenagers on the streets
(8)	Burg	Burglary
(9)	None	None of these
(10)	DontK	Don't know

M352_2a

SHOWCARD C352_2

I'm going to read out a list of problems you may encounter in your local area. By 'your local area', I mean within a 15-minute walk from your home.

Taking your answer from this card, I'd like you to tell me how much your own quality of life is affected by these problems ...

... litter/rubbish?

INTERVIEWER: Respondent to define own 'quality of life'.

(1)	NoEff	It occurs but has no effect at all
(2)	MinEff	It occurs and has a minor effect
(3)	FBigEff	It occurs and has a fairly big effect
(4)	VBEff	It occurs and has a very big effect
(5)	NotProb	This is not a problem in my local area
(6)	DontK	Don't know [Spontaneous only]

M352_2b

SHOWCARD C352_2

And how much is your own quality of life affected by ...

... vandalism and graffiti?

INTERVIEWER: Respondent to define own 'quality of life'.

(1)	NoEff	It occurs but has no effect at all
(2)	MinEff	It occurs and has a minor effect
(3)	FBigEff	It occurs and has a fairly big effect
(4)	VBEff	It occurs and has a very big effect
(5)	NotProb	This is not a problem in my local area
(6)	DontK	Don't know [Spontaneous only]

M352_2c

SHOWCARD C352_2

And how much is your own quality of life affected by ...

... abandoned cars?

INTERVIEWER: Respondent to define own 'quality of life'.

(1)	NoEff	It occurs but has no effect at all
(2)	MinEff	It occurs and has a minor effect
(3)	FBigEff	It occurs and has a fairly big effect
(4)	VBEff	It occurs and has a very big effect
(5)	NotProb	This is not a problem in my local area
(6)	DontK	Don't know [Spontaneous only]

M352_2d

SHOWCARD C352_2

And how much is your own quality of life affected by ...

... begging?

INTERVIEWER: Respondent to define own 'quality of life'.

(1)	NoEff	It occurs but has no effect at all
(2)	MinEff	It occurs and has a minor effect
(3)	FBigEff	It occurs and has a fairly big effect
(4)	VBEff	It occurs and has a very big effect
(5)	NotProb	This is not a problem in my local area
(6)	DontK	Don't know [Spontaneous only]

M352_2e

SHOWCARD C352_2

And how much is your own quality of life affected by ...

... drug use/drug dealing?

INTERVIEWER: Respondent to define own 'quality of life'.

(1)	NoEff	It occurs but has no effect at all
(2)	MinEff	It occurs and has a minor effect
(3)	FBigEff	It occurs and has a fairly big effect
(4)	VBEff	It occurs and has a very big effect
(5)	NotProb	This is not a problem in my local area
(6)	DontK	Don't know [Spontaneous only]

M352_2f

SHOWCARD C352_2

And how much is your own quality of life affected by ...

... noisy neighbours?

INTERVIEWER: Respondent to define own 'quality of life'.

(1)	NoEff	It occurs but has no effect at all
(2)	MinEff	It occurs and has a minor effect
(3)	FBigEff	It occurs and has a fairly big effect
(4)	VBEff	It occurs and has a very big effect
(5)	NotProb	This is not a problem in my local area
(6)	DontK	Don't know [Spontaneous only]

M352_2g

SHOWCARD C352_2

And how much is your own quality of life affected by ...

... rowdy teenagers on the streets?

INTERVIEWER: Respondent to define own 'quality of life'.

(1)	NoEff	It occurs but has no effect at all
(2)	MinEff	It occurs and has a minor effect
(3)	FBigEff	It occurs and has a fairly big effect
(4)	VBEff	It occurs and has a very big effect
(5)	NotProb	This is not a problem in my local area
(6)	DontK	Don't know [Spontaneous only]

M352_3

What is the worst form of anti-social behaviour in your local area? By 'your local area' I mean within a 15-minute walk from your home.

INTERVIEWER: Take respondent's definition of anti-social behaviour. There isn't a definition in use in this module.

Do not prompt. Code one only.

(1)	Litter	Litter/rubbish
(2)	Vandal	Vandalism/graffiti
(3)	Beg	Begging
(4)	Drugs	Drug use/dealing
(5)	NNbours	Noisy neighbours
(6)	Teens	Rowdy teenagers on the street
(7)	Drink	People drunk/drinking in public places
(8)	Cars	Abandoned/burnt-out vehicles
(9)	Other	Other [Please specify]
(10)	None	There isn't any form of anti-social behaviour in the area
(11)	DontK	Don't know

Ask if: M352_3 = Other

Spec_3

INTERVIEWER: Please record other type of anti-social behaviour.

M352_4

Should the police do more to tackle anti-social behaviour in your local area?

INTERVIEWER: If respondent says 'yes', please prompt 'a lot more or a little more'.

(1)	Lot	Yes – a lot more
(2)	Little	Yes – a little more

(3) NoMore No
(4) DontK Don't know

M352_5

Should the local council do more to tackle anti-social behaviour in your local area?

INTERVIEWER: If respondent says 'yes', please prompt 'a lot more or a little more'.

(1) Lot Yes – a lot more
(2) Little Yes – a little more
(3) NoMore No
(4) DontK Don't know

M352_6

Should any other groups or organisations do more to tackle anti-social behaviour in your local area?

INTERVIEWER: If respondent says 'yes', please prompt 'a lot more or a little more'.

(1) Lot Yes – a lot more
(2) Little Yes – a little more
(3) NoMore No
(4) DontK Don't know

Ask if: (M352_6 = Lot) OR (M352_6 = Little)

M352_7

Which groups or organisations?

Open response

M352_8

Have you heard of anti-social behaviour orders (or ASBOs)?

(1) Yes Yes
(2) No No
(3) DontK Don't know

M352_9

The Courts can impose anti-social behaviour orders, ASBOs, on anyone over the age of 10 who has been committing anti-social behaviour. ASBOs require these people to keep out of specified areas and/or stop behaving in specified ways. If the person ignores these conditions, they can be sent to prison/a young offenders' institution for up to five years.

M352_10

SHOWCARD C352_10

How effective do you think ASBOs will be in dealing with very disruptive neighbours?

(1)	VEff	Very effective
(2)	QEff	Quite effective
(3)	NVEff	Not very effective
(4)	NotEff	Not at all effective
(5)	DontK	Don't know [Spontaneous only]

M352_11

SHOWCARD C352_10

How effective do you think ASBOs will be in dealing with groups of youths who disrupt their local neighbourhood?

(1)	VEff	Very effective
(2)	QEff	Quite effective
(3)	NVEff	Not very effective
(4)	NotEff	Not at all effective
(5)	DontK	Don't know [Spontaneous only]

M352_12

SHOWCARD C352_12

Taking your answer from this card, which of these, if any, do you think are the three main causes of anti-social behaviour committed by young people today?

INTERVIEWER: Code main three.

SET [3] OF

(1)	Boredom	Boredom/not enough for young people to do
(2)	PrPar	Poor parenting
(3)	PrDisc	Poor discipline at school
(4)	InEfPol	Ineffective policing
(5)	Poverty	Poverty and deprivation
(6)	AlcDrug	Alcohol and drugs
(7)	NoJobs	A lack of local jobs
(8)	NoResp	Low respect for others
(9)	None	None of these
(10)	DontK	Don't know [Spontaneous only]

M352_13

If there was more money in your local area to spend on tackling anti-social behaviour within all age groups, do you think it should be spent on ...

Running prompt

(1)	ToughAct	Tough action against people committing anti-social behaviour, or
(2)	PrevAct	Preventative action to deal with the causes of anti-social behaviour?
(3)	Both	Both [Spontaneous only]
(4)	Other	Other [SPECIFY] [Spontaneous only]
(5)	Nothing	Nothing [Spontaneous only]
(6)	DontK	Don't know [Spontaneous only]

Ask if: M352_13 = Other

Spec_4

INTERVIEWER: Please record other activity where money should be spent on.

B

Appendix B: The case-study neighbourhoods

This appendix provides brief descriptions of the three case-study neighbourhoods, and the ASB initiatives in each. We found it difficult to map the work on ASB being carried out by local authorities and other responsible agencies. The problem lay in the very wide range of initiatives that had *some* relevance to ASB. Not only the police but local education authorities and schools, youth services, social services departments and primary care trusts all share significant responsibilities for responding to forms of ASB.

Southcity

The Southcity neighbourhood is in an inner London borough. It is particularly disadvantaged and has attracted funding from various regeneration and development streams. Housing provision is largely in the form of local-authority-owned estates, including some high-rise blocks. The population is ethnically mixed (26% BME), including a particularly distinct Somali group of residents. According to a report produced as part of the neighbourhood regeneration strategy, the area suffers from an accumulation of problems that make it particularly deprived:

> The design of the housing estates has led to feelings of separation. This has been compounded by the lack of local employment facilities and the need to rely on poor public transport facilities.... In particular this area suffers from high levels of crime, much of which is thought to go unreported and is not reflected in published statistics. [The area] exhibits all the classic symptoms of social exclusion (Ove Arup, 2000).

The local authority has developed a reputation for being tough on enforcement, for example, by being one of the top areas in the country for issuing ASBOs, and by being one of the first to trial the new dispersal powers in 2004. By June 2004, over 80 ASBOs had been issued in the borough, although just two of these were within the Southcity neighbourhood.[1]

The high numbers of ASBOs across the borough are largely due to its acute drugs problem. By April 2004, 60% of its ASBOs related to drug users or dealers, of which only 3% were for borough residents.[2] The borough's main centre has been a magnet for drug users and dealers for some years; however, tough enforcement strategies, involving a high police presence, have displaced some of the problems to neighbouring areas, including the Southcity neighbourhood. There is one particular street and a market in Southcity where local residents are concerned about visible drug dealing and using. Southcity also has a large 'youth nuisance' problem. For instance, according to March 2004 figures, Southcity had the highest number of calls to the borough for youth nuisance with 74 calls.[3] The area also has a particular problem with street drinkers.

There are numerous projects active in the neighbourhood that may have a bearing on ASB.

---

1 The borough has a target of 16 ASBOs per year, but is securing around 40 per year, largely due to the area's drug problems. According to the borough's ASB coordinator, only one youth ASBO was gained in the last year (although figures may be higher as he does not deal with post-conviction ASBOs).

2 Borough Anti-Social Behaviour Scrutiny Panel, April 2004.

3 Borough Anti-Social Behaviour Scrutiny Panel, June 2004.

A summary of the principal activities is given here.

Neighbourhood Management Pathfinder

This is funded by the Neighbourhood Renewal Fund, with a remit to bring together service providers and residents in the area so that they work together to provide a more efficient, effective service (see ODPM, 2004). The project is in its third year with the intention to last for seven years. Priority issues are to tackle ASB and crime. For ASB, the Pathfinder project includes behaviour associated with drug use, chaotic lifestyles and gangs. Indicators for measuring ASB are being developed. Along with funding various community safety posts, the project has funded private security guard/dog patrols[4] in order to discourage youth problems and assist with the evacuation of parks at closing times. The partnership has employed a play worker to coordinate work in the area with young people, and to identify any gaps in provision. Pathfinder has also funded two PCSO posts.

Safer Neighbourhoods Team

The neighbourhood is one of the trial sites for the Metropolitan Police's new 'Safer Neighbourhoods Teams'. This is a new form of community-based policing where each neighbourhood is allocated a dedicated Sergeant, two constables and three PCSOs. The aim is to provide a more visible police presence in the community. Although in this instance the officers are based at a police station outside of the neighbourhood, they do make regular patrols in the area and an on-site office from which they can operate is being developed.

Youth Inclusion Support Panel (YISP)

This panel works closely with the YOT. Their purpose of the panel is to develop specific plans for individual 'troublemakers' in the area. Recommendations could include Acceptable Behaviour Contracts (ABCs). The current system is a 'two strikes and you're out' approach. If an ABC is breached there is a yellow warning, followed by a red and then an ASBO application will be considered.

Environmental Work

Street cleaning teams are active in the area giving priority to the removal of offensive graffiti within 24 hours. There are targets to remove abandoned vehicles[5] within two days. Noise Patrols operate borough-wide and are most active on the weekends. Some council housing estates have been gated following requests from residents with the aim to prevent robbery and ASB.

Other work

There are many other activities that could conceivably impact on ASB. Most directly, a dispersal order has been trialled in the borough, the area of coverage overlapping with one part of Southcity. There is also a variety of provision for young people and parents, including the work of the YOT, SureStart, Connexions, the Red Hot Greens project that gives a group of young people a 'voice' in what goes on in the area, various football tournaments and the Bright Sparks initiative (dealing with fireworks problems). There are various organisations and charities active in the area dealing with drug problems. The borough runs a mediation service that can help with some neighbour disputes.

Westerncity

The Westerncity neighbourhood is in a city in South Wales. Like Southcity, it has high levels of deprivation but, unlike Southcity, it is located in the outer suburbs. While the neighbourhood has some privately owned housing, most provision is in the form of low-rise council housing estates. The area has over the last few decades suffered from high unemployment. The area is predominantly White, although there are a few BME asylum seekers living in the area. During the 1990s Westerncity suffered particularly badly from joyriding and related ASB. A neighbouring beauty-spot regularly saw cars being burnt out and even the open ground itself was regularly set alight each summer. Over the last two to three

[4] Managed by the Leisure and Community Services Department

[5] According to the area housing manager these are currently more likely to be stolen or smashed-up mopeds/scooters.

years the car crime problem has diminished – although some residents fear that it may come back.

Problems of youth ASB are thought to be severe. Symptoms include young people 'hanging about' and drinking alcohol. There is some drugs use, but the problem is much smaller than in Southcity. The local CDRP has adopted a 'softly-softly' approach to ASB enforcement. Like Southcity, there is a graduated response with ASBOs regarded as a last resort; unlike Southcity, this has led to far fewer ASBOs. By mid-2004, there had been just three ASBOs[6] in the whole city and none in the Westerncity neighbourhood. Activity taking place in Westerncity that could impact on ASB includes the following:

Communities that Care (CTC)

This is a programme put in place by a national charity set up in 1997 by the Joseph Rowntree Foundation; it is a development of the American CTC model.[7] It was set up in Westerncity in 2000 and is a long-term, 10-year programme (Fairnington, 2004). It is community-based and aims to build 'safer, healthier and more cohesive communities where children and young people are valued and able to achieve their full potential'. It is based on evidence derived from analysis of 'risk' and 'protective' factors, as identified by local people and professionals working together. The CTC coordinator acts as a local broker, aiming to link local projects – or ideas for projects – with funding sources.

Funding by Communities First (Welsh Assembly Government)

The Communities First project started in 2004; its aims are community engagement and regeneration. So far, a 'Big Brother' diary room[8] has been tried where members of the community can voice their concerns and wishes for the neighbourhood. Other ways of gaining community engagement have been through, for example, bingo sessions for older residents and a fashion show for children.

CDRP anti-social behaviour structure

The CDRP follows a graduated response to ASB, with ASBOs regarded as the last resort – a sign that they have failed to prevent the problem from escalating. The four-point plan involves the sending of first and second letters to perpetrators, the second being accompanied by a visit. On the third referral there is a further letter and a case conference – the 'problem solving group' – that meets to discuss the case and an ABC or other suitable intervention can be recommended. (In severe cases, the early stages can be by-passed.) On the fourth referral an ASBO is an option. From 1 January 2003 to 15 July 2004, 1,170 first letters were sent out across the whole city and one ASBO was issued. In the Westerncity neighbourhood, 73 first letters were sent out and no ASBOs issued.

Local 'community house'

A local resident – with help from other volunteers – provides a community house that acts as a drop-in centre for local parents, children and other residents. The house is provided by the local authority at a minimum rent.

Regeneration of property

A proportion of the pre-war local authority housing stock has been refurbished with the result that local residents now take greater care over their properties with, according to one resident, greater pride in maintaining such things as gardens.

Early intervention work

There are two early intervention programmes running in Westerncity. The first is a development of the American High/Scope[9] approach to pre-school education based at the [Westerncity] Family Centre, where sessions are 'child-led'. They are based on routine and

6 Two were on persistent offenders (both young males) and one a post-conviction ASBO on a male in his mid-30s. This was imposed by the court rather than being sought by the Partnership.

7 See eg France and Crow (2001) and Fairnington (2004).

8 The area's young people were far more enthusiastic about this than the rest of the population.

9 See www.highscope.org

develop ideas of responsibility, choice and consequence. The second is Project Charlie, which is based at a local primary school. This encourages the development of cognitive skills and problem solving. The aim is to encourage young people to make decisions and resist peer pressure.

Other work

There are numerous other projects that could have an impact on ASB. The area has a 'Healthy Living Centre' – funded by a New Opportunities Fund – that runs peer-led initiatives on health issues; for example, looking at issues around tobacco and alcohol with young people. There is also the work of the YOT and the Welsh equivalent of the English SureStart/Connexions provision – Cymorth and the Children and Youth Partnership Framework. There are various environmental targets for dealing with graffiti and abandoned vehicles. Local policing is provided by a community officer and two PCSOs. The local authority housing department – through their Neighbourhood Support Unit – provides daily van patrols that target hotspots of concern across the city.

Midcity

The Midcity neighbourhood forms part of the outer suburbs of an East Midlands city. The area is similar to Westerncity in that it is formed of deprived edge-of-city council estates – plus some private provision. The population is predominantly White, although around 15 per cent are from BME groups. Like Westerncity the area has over the last 10 years had some serious problems with joyriding and associated youth ASB. The area still suffers from these problems on a daily basis. The area has three **main** estates, each with a different character. Estate A has a high concentration of young people and consequently has the most acute problems of youth ASB. Estate B has large numbers of retired people and Estate C mainly consists of families. Due to the joyriding and ASB problems, Estate A has very intense CCTV coverage and 'traffic calming' which, according to some, shifts the problems onto the other estates. Others interviewed think these measures just present more of a challenge to the young people. Drug use and dealing are increasingly a problem in the area. A recent additional and related concern has been increases in gun crime across the city, including some instances in the Midcity area.

The approach adopted by the CDRP is becoming more enforcement focused. In 2003/04, 10 ASBOs were issued across the city (excluding post-conviction ASBOs that are directly imposed by the courts); and by August 2004 there had been 17 applications for dispersal orders across the city. In the Midcity neighbourhood, five stand-alone ASBOs have been issued over the past five years, along with a number of post-conviction ASBOs; at the time of writing, there are around 20 individuals under consideration for ASBOs in Midcity. The Midcity neighbourhood has also had two ABCs and the housing department has sought approximately 20 possession orders per year. There is currently one dispersal order in operation in Midcity (Estate A). Local policing is by a combination of PCSOs and community constables; additional patrols are provided by neighbourhood wardens funded by the local authority. As with the other two sites, there is a range of activity taking place in the Midcity neighbourhood that could impact on ASB. These are listed below.

Area Team and Community Safety Panel

The aim of this work – managed by the local authority Neighbourhood Services – is to improve the health, well-being and education of people living in the Midcity area. The work feeds into the city-wide 'Respect' campaign (see below). The Midcity Area Team has gained funding for various environmental improvements aimed at reducing crime and ASB – including CCTV and other situational measures. They have also worked with Crime Concern to try and improve provision for young people in the area and have set up a local youth club. Following consultation with community members and local agencies, ASB has been identified as a key issue for the area. As such, an Area ASB Strategy is being put together.[10] A Community Safety Panel is being formed with the aim to be:

[10] The [Midcity] Area Team, in partnership with Crime Concern, organised an 'ASB Day' in July 2004 when individuals could contribute to the strategy priorities.

- An inclusive forum for local problem-solving;
- An opportunity to influence policy and access funding;
- A partnership to facilitate community engagement;
- A partnership to build on existing social capital; and
- A mechanism to reduce crime and anti-social behaviour.[11]

Various community groups and local partners have been identified that will form the forum.

The city-wide 'Respect' campaign

This is the city-wide agenda for reducing ASB. The campaign's focus is on neighbourhoods, although a lot of current emphasis is on the city centre, looking particularly at problems of prostitution and street begging. Linked to this has been a '100 Day Clean-up Campaign', although again, this work was largely city-centre focused.

Local housing office ASB 'Task Force' teams

From late 2004 onwards each local housing area has had a dedicated ASB 'Task Force' Team. There are four across the city, each comprising two local authority ASB officers, two police officers, two PCSOs and two local authority wardens.

Working with young people and families

Various organisations and agencies provide for young people, children and parents. Key providers are SureStart, Connexions, the YOT, YISP and the local Family Centre which works with children aged four to 13. Additional youth work is provided which is funded by the Single Regeneration Budget.

Other work

Other enforcement work is currently focused on post-conviction ASBOs, in the belief that they are easier and cheaper to obtain than a stand-alone order. At August 2004 there were four post-conviction ASBOs being sought for perpetrators in the Midcity neighbourhood and a further two across the city; one was for a prolific shoplifter, one for a car thief; and the rest were 'prolific in everything they do, just harassing folk, general nuisance, burglary, theft'. (local sergeant)

[11] Report to the city's Corporate Director of Neighbourhood Services (*Anti-Social Behaviour Strategy Update*, September 2004).

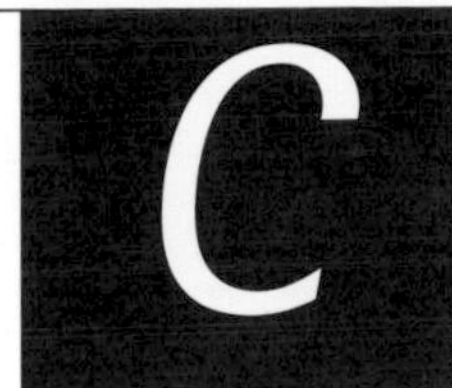

Appendix C: Logistic regression models

Logistic regression has been used extensively in criminological research (for example, Clancy et al, 2001; FitzGerald et al, 2002). It is a multivariate technique in which statistical relationships between an independent variable (for example, age or ethnicity) and a dependent variable (for example, thinks 'rowdy teenagers on the streets' is the worst form of ASB in my area) can be determined, once possible associations with other variables have been taken into account. For example, income and education status may predict experience of ASB, but they may also be related to one another. Logistic regression means that a correlation between income and experience of ASB – in its own right – can be tested. However, the model does only indicate whether there is a case for an effect on outcome, and does not prove that causal links exist. As with the majority of survey data, the regression models only explain a small part of the variance in the dependent variables as the dataset does not capture all information that may be relevant.

Table A1: Logistic regression model for predictors of: 'rowdy teenagers on the streets' is the worst form of ASB in my area

Factor	B	Exp (â)	Significance
Significant			
Retirement age	–0.602	0.548	$p<0.01$
White	0.484	1.622	$p<0.05$
Non-significant			
Children in household[a]; Rents LA/HA; Owns outright/with mortgage; Aged 16-30; Aged 18-30; Gender; Lone parent with dependent child; One person household; Have degree or equivalent; Have no qualifications; Live in London Govt. Office region			
Weighted data, unweighted n=1,583 (rowdy teenagers worst form of ASB n=452)			

Notes: [a]'Children in household' was approaching significance. Refusals and 'don't knows' are excluded from the analysis.

Table A2: Logistic regression model for predictors of: there isn't any form of ASB in the area

Factor	B	Exp (â)	Significance
Significant			
Retirement age	0.575	1.776	$p<0.01$
Have degree or equivalent	–0.698	0.497	$p<0.01$
Gender (male)	0.345	0.708	$p<0.05$
Non-significant			
Children in household; White; BME/mixed; Rents LA/HA; Owns outright/with mortgage; Aged 16-30; Aged 18-30; Lone parent with dependent child; One person household; Have no qualifications; Live in London Govt. Office region			
Weighted data, unweighted n=1,597 (isn't any form of ASB n=291)			

Note: Refusals and 'don't knows' are excluded from the analysis.

Table A3: Logistic regression model for predictors of: vandalism/graffiti is the worst form of ASB in my area

Factor	B	Exp (â)	Significance
Significant			
Rents LA/HA	1.310	3.707	$p<0.05$
Owns outright/has mortgage	1.114	3.046	$p<0.05$
Non-significant			
Have no qualifications; Have degree or equivalent; Gender; White; BME/mixed; Children in household; Rents LA/HA; Owns outright/with mortgage; Aged 18-30; Aged 16-30; Retired; Lone parent with dependent child; One person household; Live in London Govt. Office region			
Weighted data, unweighted n=1,596 (drug use/dealing worst form of ASB n=142)			

Note: Refusals and 'don't knows' are excluded from the analysis.

Table A4: Logistic regression model for predictors of: litter/rubbish is the worst form of ASB in my area

Factor	B	Exp (â)	Significance
Significant			
Retirement age	0.768	2.155	$p<0.01$
Have degree or equivalent	0.728	2.072	$p<0.01$
Non-significant			
Gender; Children in household; White; BME/mixed; Rents LA/HA; Owns outright/with mortgage; Aged 16-30; Aged 18-30; Lone parent with dependent child; One person household; Have no qualifications; Live in London Govt. Office region			
Weighted data, unweighted n=1,597 (litter/rubbish worst form of ASB n=138)			

Note: Refusals and 'don't knows' are excluded from the analysis.

Table A5: Logistic regression model for predictors of: drug use/dealing being the worst form of ASB in my area

Factor	B	Exp (â)	Significance
Significant			
BME/mixed	0.985	2.677	$p<0.01$
Aged 16-30	0.580	1.786	$p<0.01$
Have degree or equivalent	-0.692	0.501	$p<0.05$
Non-significant			
Have no qualifications; Gender; Children in household; Rents LA/HA; Owns outright/with mortgage; Aged 18-30; Retired; Lone parent with dependent child; One person household; Live in London Govt. Office region			
Weighted data, unweighted n=1,583 (drug use/dealing worst form of ASB n=127)			

Note: Refusals and 'don't knows' are excluded from the analysis.

Table A6: Logistic regression model for predictors of: rowdy teenagers on the streets having a fairly big/very big affect on quality of life

Factor	B	Exp (â)	Significance
Significant			
Retirement age	–0.654	0.520	$p<0.01$
Live in London Govt. Office region	0.687	1.988	$p<0.01$
Rents LA/HA	0.564	1.758	$p<0.01$
Aged 18 to 30	0.503	1.654	$p<0.01$
Have no qualifications	0.348	1.416	$p<0.05$
BME/mixed	0.499	1.647	$p<0.05$
Non-significant			
Children in household; Owns outright/with mortgage; Aged 16-30; Aged 16-18; Gender; Lone parent with dependent child; One person household; Have degree or equivalent			
Weighted data, unweighted n=1,661 (rowdy teenagers fairly big/very big affect n=325)			

Note: 'Don't knows' are excluded from the analysis.

Table A7: Logistic regression model for predictors of: drug use/dealing having a fairly big/very big affect on quality of life

Factor	B	Exp (â)	Significance
Significant			
BME/mixed	1.116	3.054	$p<0.01$
Retirement age	–0.885	0.413	$p<0.01$
Rents LA/HA	0.658	1.931	$p<0.01$
Have degree or equivalent	–0.690	0.501	$p<0.01$
Have no qualifications	0.350	1.419	$p<0.05$
Non-significant			
Children in household; Owns outright/with mortgage; Aged 16-30; Aged 16-18; Aged 18-30; Gender; Lone parent with dependent child; One person household; Live in London Govt. Office region			
Weighted data, unweighted n=1,579 (drug use/dealing fairly big/very big affect n=281)			

Note: 'Don't knows' are excluded from the analysis.

Table A8: Logistic regression model for predictors of: vandalism/graffiti having a fairly big/very big affect on quality of life

Factor	B	Exp (â)	Significance
Significant			
Have no qualifications	0.651	1.918	$p<0.01$
Live in London Govt. Office region	0.653	1.921	$p<0.01$
Aged 18 to 30	0.428	1.534	$p<0.05$
Non-significant			
Children in household; Rents LA/HA; Owns outright/with mortgage; Retirement age; Aged 16-30; Aged 16-18; Ethnicity; Gender; Lone parent with dependent child; One person household; Have degree or equivalent			
Weighted data, unweighted n=1,672 (vandalism/graffiti fairly big/very big affect n=281)			

Note: 'Don't knows' are excluded from the analysis.

Table A9: Logistic regression model for predictors of: litter/rubbish having a fairly big/very big affect on quality of life

Factor	B	Exp (â)	Significance
Significant			
Live in London Govt. Office region	0.920	2.510	$p<0.01$
Have no qualifications	0.351	1.420	$p<0.01$
Non-significant			
Children in household; Rents LA/HA; Owns outright/with mortgage; Retirement age; Aged 16-30; Aged 18-30; Aged 16-18; Ethnicity; Gender; Lone parent with dependent child; One person household; Have degree or equivalent			
Weighted data, unweighted n=1,672 (litter/rubbish fairly big/very big affect n=295)			

Note: 'Don't knows' are excluded from the analysis.

Table A10: Logistic regression model for predictors of: money should be spent on tough action against people committing ASB

Factor	B	Exp (â)	Significance
Significant			
Retirement age	0.421	1.523	$p<0.01$
Gender (male)	0.356	1.427	$p<0.01$
Owns outright/with mortgage	–0.356	0.701	$p<0.05$
Have degree or equivalent	–0.502	0.605	$p<0.05$
Non-significant			
Have no qualifications; Children in household; Rents LA/HA; Aged 18-30; Aged 16-18; Aged 16-30; Ethnicity; Lone parent with dependent child; One person household; Live in London Govt. Office region			
Weighted data, unweighted n=1,653 (tough action n=328)			

Note: 'Don't knows' are excluded from the analysis.

Table A11: Logistic regression model for predictors of: money should be spent on preventative action to deal with the causes of ASB

Factor	B	Exp (â)	Significance
Significant			
Gender (female)	0.341	1.406	$p<0.01$
Live in London Govt. Office region	–0.434	0.646	$p<0.05$
Have degree or equivalent	0.375	1.455	$p<0.05$
Have no qualifications	–0.250	0.779	$p<0.05$
Non-significant			
Children in household; Rents LA/HA; Owns outright/with mortgage; Retirement age; Aged 18-30; Aged 16-18; Aged 16-30; Ethnicity; Lone parent with dependent child; One person household;			
Weighted data, unweighted n=1,654 (preventative action n=1,117)			

Note: 'Don't knows' are excluded from the analysis.